The War Within

What I Witnessed From Inside the Capitol on Jan. 6

The War Within

What I Witnessed From Inside the Capitol on Jan. 6

Jamie Stiehm

Creators Publishing
Hermosa Beach, CA

The War Within: What I Witnessed From Inside the Capitol on Jan. 6
Copyright © 2024 CREATORS PUBLISHING
All rights reserved. No part of this book may be reproduced or transmitted in any form or by any means, electronic or mechanical, including photocopying, recording or by any information storage and retrieval system, without permission in writing from the author.

Cover art by Rishikumar Thakur

CREATORS PUBLISHING
737 3rd St
Hermosa Beach, CA 90254
310-337-7003

Although the author and publisher have made every effort to ensure that the information in this book was correct at press time, the author and publisher do not assume and hereby disclaim any liability to any party for any loss, damage or disruption caused by errors or omissions, whether such errors or omissions result from negligence, accident or any other cause.

ISBN (print): 978-1-962693-08-0

First Edition
Printed in the United States of America
1 3 5 7 9 10 8 6 4 2

A Note From the Publisher

Our goal is to make you think. We want you to react. We want you to respond.

Since 1987, the writers we represent and publish start discussions, arguments and even controversies. Love them or hate them, you can't ignore them.

Beginning with print and evolving into digital, Creators has been at the forefront of the media industry. We have been disrupting the status quo since our company was founded on the premise that creators should own their work, characters and ideas. Decades later, we continue to evolve as society pushes forward and technology changes.

At Creators, we support creators.

—Creators Publishing

Contents

Introduction	1
Prelude	6
Trump Will Never Surrender, Just Like Jefferson Davis	7
The Bitter With the Sweet, Served at Thanksgiving	10
In Private Sieges, Missing Public Squares	13
Life in a Dickensian-Trumpian Tale of Hard Times — at Christmas	16
On a Long, Dark Night, Congress Caught Doing Something Right	19
Lord, What Did We Do To Deserve 2020?	22
Crisis	25
A Desperate Duel for Democracy	26
'Capitolnacht': Darkness on the Nation's Doorstep	29
Racist Mobs Rage All Over American History	32
The Mob Cannot Go Home Again	35
Profiles in Cowardice: The Mob Still Haunts the Halls	38
The Capitol Trial on the President's Riot	41
Painting Parallels of Presidents' Civil Wars	44
Biden Knows His Task: To Repair Broken Parts and Hearts	47
Don't Fence the Capitol In or Out	50
Democrats Seize the Spring and March With More Spirit	53
The Plagues of Democracy — God Help Us	56
A Love Lost: The Senate and Me	59
The 4th Brings Us Back to Each Other	62
The Search for Truth on Jan. 6 Brings Tears	65
Two Californias Clash in a Divided House: Pelosi Versus McCarthy	68
The Tragic March of 2021: Will It Ever End Well	71
Diary Notes: Washington Puts a Dark Past To Rest	74

Biden Needs to Keep Away Skunks and Mobs ... 77
At Thanksgiving, Democracy on the Table ... 80
The Trump Contagion Still Spreading ... 83

Aftermath ... 86

Seven Senators Who Go Back to Civil War Days ... 87
The Kindness of New Yorkers as Christmas Came Near ... 90
The 21st Century: A Flop So Far ... 93
Senate Sets Stage for Showdown on Voting Rights ... 96
Biden Meets the Moment in the House ... 99
Trump Pecked and Plucked, Feather by Feather ... 102
Pelosi Makes Most of History Every Day ... 105
Three Stages of Violence: Hollywood, Washington, Ukraine ... 108
April Brings Uncertain Things, Now and Then ... 111
How Far the Party Fell Into the Abyss: From Hatch to McCarthy ... 114
A Sad Situation, the State of the Nation ... 117
Midterms: The First Stress Test for Democracy (And Trump) Since Jan. 6 ... 120
Sharing a Cell in History Hell: Trump and Nixon ... 123
Athens and America: Helpful Hints for the Fix We're In ... 126
A Pearl of Hope For An Unhappy Birthday ... 129
Trump's Knots and Dots: It's All Over ... 132
A Midsummer's Nightmare: Onstage in Washington ... 135
Field Notes: The Summer Burn Of '22 ... 138
Our Towns: Jan. 6 Justice Done — And Alive Again ... 141
Why Trump Talks Nonstop About Witch Hunts ... 144
The Good, the Bad and the Ugly ... 147
Two Blows in One Night to Democracy ... 150
Voters Verdict: End of The Trump Era ... 153
Giving Thanks to Madam Speaker ... 156
A Dearth — Or Death — Of Charm in the Capitol ... 159
Washington Wakes up for the Holidays ... 162

The Mob Came for Me, Thee and Democracy: A Vindication	165
The House Showed the Senate the Way, Time After Time	168
Full House Theater: An American Tragedy	171
The Three Women of San Francisco	174
Brash Young Governor Trumps Trump	177
The Day That Justice Comes for Trump, One Senator Never Surrenders	180
Gathering Storm Shows House Republicans Have No Limits	183
The Best of the Worst: Republicans for President	186
From Capitol to Courthouse: Like a Vision	189
In Trump They Trust: Bread and Circuses	193
Justice For a January Day, At Last	196
About the Author	199

Introduction

Suddenly, the sacred house of democracy was under siege. And I was in it, seated in the press gallery of the House of Representatives. The date now engraved on history: January 6, 2021, a winter Wednesday afternoon in Washington.

Crossing the grounds of the U.S. Capitol from Union Station, my work took me to cover the constitutional ritual of Congress confirming the Electoral Count that sealed Joe Biden's victory in the 2020 election over the loser, Donald Trump.

Looking back, both chambers of Congress were full, making the Senate and House captive to a conspiracy hatched by violent extremists on the Internet, from all corners of the country. President Trump had invited his followers to the "wild" day.

Just after noon, Trump addressed a throng of supporters, some armed. He incited and invited them to march on the National Mall, heading toward the Capitol. And it's not a long walk.

As they advanced, I made my was like any other day on Capitol Hill. This was my chosen beat. I loved this place. George Washington laid the cornerstone.

Except a woman Capitol Police officer and I exchanged glances and she said I should leave before dark.

Trouble brewed. You could smell it like strong coffee. As I approached the House side, I heard a raucous "pledge of allegiance" from a gathering. The pledge was to "DONALD TRUMP."

I called my sister Carrie in California and said, "Something bad is going to happen. I don't know what, but something."

Foreboding aside, I made it to the third-floor press gallery. Covid had reduced the usual number of reporters. We were given N95 masks, only 25 or 30 of us. Business as usual, right? From the overhead gallery, we observed the House floor.

I chose the House chamber because Speaker Nancy Pelosi presided over the count. There was never a dull moment with her. I had recently interviewed her on woman suffrage. Besides, the House is always more diverse and colorful than the Senate.

Vice President Mike Pence presided on the Senate side. These two leaders were first and second in line to the presidency. They would each come under fire, pursued in a hunt, in short order. Little did we know.

Clearly, not all 435 members came to the House floor. Covid had reduced their numbers to about half. Some stayed in their offices or homes to vote remotely. Thank goodness.

Freshman Lauren Boebart, (R- Colo.) stood up to brag to "Madam Speaker" that she carried a gun – not then and there, but in general. A stunning harbinger of what was about to break out after the count began.

First a nameless voice piped in: "An individual has breached the Rotunda." Pelosi kept the vote count going, state by state. Then she was spirited out of the chamber. We could not see that from above.

To this day, I wish the announcer had told us the truth. This crisis was no "individual" but a heaving mass, shoving and punching police officers, yelling racist slurs to Black officers.

As the portrait of Moses looked down, we heard pounding footsteps, furious jeers, glass breaking on marble halls. Then right below us, by the ornate Speaker's lobby, a single gunshot. It landed like a raven in the room.

At this point, we were all in the dark: who was shooting who?

The air fogged from tear gas. Someone told us to put on "escape hoods" and crawl to a secret staircase. But the doors were locked in a desperate moment. Clearly, the Capitol police had lost control of the building, while the mob seemed to know where they were going. They had a plan.

Then time froze as strange, bearded faces poked through

jagged glass on a main entrance door into the House floor. Two congressmen, a former Army Ranger and a former NFL linebacker, took their jackets off to fight with their bare hands. One felt he'd never get to see his firstborn son, due in weeks.

Four detectives held the bearded guys at gunpoint, should they try to break and rush the House door. No telling how long that lasted. Nobody could take their eyes from the silent stand-off directly across the floor from us. That held our fate.

My sister Carrie called to say, "You are in danger." Four quiet words. She did not say 30,000 swarmed outside the Capitol, scaling walls and storming doors, determined to overturn the election.

In a flash came the first time in my life that I thought it was over. I always thought I'd live to be 100 like my great-grandfather, made of strong midwestern stock.

On September 11th, the Capitol was spared because the "fourth plane" crashed to the ground. The Capitol, twenty minutes away, was the perfect target in a cloudless sky. Knowing this, would the Capitol itself survive this day?

I couldn't let myself go there. I had to stay focused on right here and now.

But the Sept. 11th terrorist hijackers were an external threat, most of them Saudis. The difference was, Americans were attacking their own government in *a war within* for the first time ever.

We took off our shoes and went single file along the rows of seats to the one unlocked door, leading to a secret staircase to a tunnel. I was breathing hard, walking with a senior Democratic lawmaker, Marcy Kaptur of Ohio. Neither of us wore escape hoods.

Her face and pearls were perfectly composed, so I asked her, "Congresswoman, why are you so calm?"

"I've had a lot of hardship in my life," she said. I felt a little bit better.

As long as the mob didn't come at us from the tunnel's

other end, I figured, we would be all right.

The second part of the day was spent in lockdown in a large House office building. The press mingled with the Capitol labor force, who keep the building, even the basement floors, pristine. Their work was being trammeled and ransacked as we spoke.

"It hurts your heart," one craftsman said slowly. The magnificent historical murals, sculptures, drapes, chandeliers, Italianate frescos and tile floors were at the mercy of the mob.

I gave an interview to the BBC News radio and felt myself coming back to life from a state of shock. Anger and astonishment awakened me.

Hours passed, as photographers and other journalists joked in gallows humor. We missed the Vietnam War, but here we were. A CNN producer said she ducked into a senator's hideaway during the rampage – he was gone with the other 99.

Meanwhile, Trump watched the storming with schadenfreude. He loves large crowd sizes and high ratings. Trump ignored pleas to call off the violent siege, which went on till late in the day, almost dark.

Maybe he was having the time of his life.

Police casualties climbed to 150. The city Metropolitan police force rushed to help defend against the attackers. Frankly, without the 800 well-trained city cops, the blood bath would have soaked many more of us.

On the Senate side, the mob broke into the chamber and 100 senators fled for their life. Tommy Tuberville, an Alabama freshman (R) told me Trump called him at that very moment. "I was the last guy out."

Trump wanted a status report. Did he want to know if Pence still in there safe from harm while a gallows was set up for him?

A gruesome thought for a perfectly nice democracy with a pretty good constitution, always with a peaceful transfer of power.

Until now.

The third part of that journey was returning to the embattled Capitol to finish the formal count. I'll always respect Pelosi and Pence for not letting the mob win.

Rudely interrupted, the House and Senate went to their respective quarters. Things were still rocky because scores of Republicans challenged the numbers. I lost track of time when the ordeal was finally over. I spoke to two senators by the Ohio Clock way past midnight.

One told me Pence was livid, "after all I've done for Trump." Another senator said, "They're playing with fire."

Gunfire.

What an irony that I covered the streets of Baltimore for seven years as a reporter and always felt safe. Yet in this citadel, we were stormed by white supremacists (including veterans) politically descended from the Ku Klux Klan. Some were literally loaded for bear, with bear spray.

Back on the House side, I struck up a conversation with a cool teenager standing by a statue of Will Rogers. "Dude, really?" he said. "A coup?" He told me his grandmother was the Speaker.

The city was under curfew, pitch black punctuated by blinking sirens and law enforcement lights. Where the FBI was that day, don't ask, but the insurrection was its massive intelligence failure. Extremist groups like the Proud Boys had open online chat rooms on Jan. 6 logistics.

The pre-dawn dark coated the air when the count was finished about 4 am. The nicest guy under the dome, a press gallery superintendent, gave me a lift home through those eerie empty streets. It felt like another country, and maybe it was.

When I hit the sheets, I lay still. When the sun at last rose, that's when I wept.

Prelude

Trump Will Never Surrender, Just Like Jefferson Davis

Nov. 11, 2020

WASHINGTON—Autumn sun lights the city after President Donald Trump lost to Joe Biden, except the civil war he started isn't over yet. The part Trump's playing in this tragic drama: the traitor, like despicable Jefferson Davis, who conducted the Civil War over slavery.

Trump's historic refusal to concede is the perfect parallel to the Confederate president, the Mississippi senator and enslaver who tore the country apart. He nearly succeeded but for prairie giant President Abraham Lincoln.

Like Trump, Davis never surrendered his white supremacist lost cause.

After the ravages of the Trump term, the American people must brace for a defiant last stand from the worst loser in the world, for history does rhyme all the time.

Even as the Civil War ended, after Richmond fell, Davis was captured in Georgia while fleeing by Union cavalry soldiers. He was dressed as a woman. By 1865, the Confederate states were weary, shattered by four years of war.

These were Trumpian red states in 2016, except Virginia. So, Davis still had his fingerprints on the American political map. The evil men do lives long after them, said Shakespeare.

Davis was imprisoned after the Civil War, a fate that may await the outgoing president. Too bad they can't be cellmates. They're soul mates.

We just got word Trump fired his Secretary of Defense, Mark Esper, because he resisted sending in the military to peaceful protests. That's more serious than the inmate running the White House asylum. There's no telling what our own hateful Confederate might do, after cutting jagged rifts of resentment across America.

House Speaker Nancy Pelosi, D-Calif., declared, "The abrupt firing of Secretary Esper is disturbing evidence that

President Trump is intent on using his final days in office to sow chaos in our American Democracy and around the world."

Heed her words. As the top Democrat who stood up to him, Pelosi knows her Trump. In the first Oval Office meeting, he claimed he won the popular vote. One of myriad lies. She confronted him in front of all his men.

Then came the House impeachment, with witnesses on presidential plotting in Ukraine.

Pelosi told the president, "All roads lead to (Vladimir) Putin." To his face.

Her ripping up his State of the Union speech was elegant resistance. Trump hasn't spoken to the Speaker since.

To review, the rule with Trump is there are no rules. Second, he desperately has to win—and lies, cheats and steals to achieve that. Third, he does his best to bring out the worst in people, the greatest talent of these three things.

All along, he cunningly courted the "old South" block and solidified it, building racial strife. The deadly Virginia race riot in Charlottesville showed whose side he was on. He equated the sides as "very fine people."

Taking revenge, Trump could smash the body politic into smithereens. Just as Davis sowed seeds of Southern rage for a century-and-a-half toward Yankees.

Did the Civil War, North and South, ever end?

I like the symmetry of Pennsylvania and Georgia, then and now. Biden won the state where he was born, as Pennsylvania took him to the mountaintop on Saturday noon. I happened to be in Delaware, biking through pine forest and salt marshes to the ocean.

In 1863, the Battle of Gettysburg changed everything. The Union victory, after three days, happened July 4 on Pennsylvania farmland. Confederate general Robert E. Lee lost big on his Northern gambit.

A high-class traitor, Lee later showed grace in meeting Gen. Ulysses Grant for "The Surrender."

The hated phrase "Marching through Georgia" is Gen.

William Tecumseh Sherman's campaign to burn Atlanta and march to the sea, where he claimed Savannah. Sherman broke the civilian Confederacy.

At last count, Georgia is the only Deep South state Biden carried — a hopeful sign the late hero, Rep. John Lewis, D-Ga., galvanized Atlanta voters and helped racial healing in the age of Trump. The morning after his 2017 inauguration, the Rev. Jesse Jackson told me Trump was like "a Confederate." Prescient moment.

Burning candles, Davis played martyr to the bitter end of his long life.

The Bitter With the Sweet, Served at Thanksgiving

Nov. 25, 2020

WASHINGTON — Roses in the wind, waving before winter's cold comes. They signify our bittersweet November perfectly. The sky grows dark early, but with a burst of beauty on the bleak political front, thankfully.

Thanksgiving is upon us, because a great president renewed the pilgrims' feast and faith 400 years ago.

The anxious capital is counting the days to Joe Biden's presidency. The torch will be passed on Jan. 20. We're also counting coronavirus cases, past the 12 million mark now. Bittersweet doesn't get better than that.

November calls up memory of past presidencies.

For Americans older than 3 on Nov. 22, 1963, the tragic murder of John F. Kennedy in Dallas is lodged like a bullet in their brains. Kennedy was so witty, youthful, bright, charming and eloquent that it didn't seem possible that he was gone in a flash. Men, women and children wept. For the rest of time, they could say where they were frozen when they heard the news.

The early '60s, bright days, were shattered.

Passing strange that the Yankee president, dashing Jack Kennedy of Massachusetts, was slain in what was the largest Confederate state, known for a swagger. Blood spilled on Mrs. Kennedy's pink dress and history's hands.

On Nov. 19, 1863, President Abraham Lincoln had traveled to Pennsylvania to deliver a brief address at the Gettysburg battlefield. Remarkably, it was 100 Novembers apart from the 1963 assassination.

Presidents Kennedy and Lincoln are tied together in an autumnal rhyme.

The three-day July battle in rolling farm country, epic in its casualties, turned the Civil War. The Union army won, thankfully, against Gen. Robert E. Lee's forces, which had never ventured so far north. It was a matter of time before the Confederacy surrendered in April 1865, if it ever did.

In the darkest days, Lincoln's words at Gettysburg changed the war's meaning in majestic presidential prose. It wasn't only the country map anymore, but "a new birth of freedom," declared the man who freed 4 million enslaved people. American democracy expanded. The somber setting spoke of the high cost in suffering and loss.

When Lincoln was murdered here one April Friday night in 1865, days after the war ended, the nation's grief was great, an ocean of tears as lilacs bloomed. He was the Civil War's final casualty.

"We want the sun to be darkened, and the moon not to give her light," Lucretia Mott, the famed Philadelphia Quaker, said. It was the first time an American president was violently cut down — by a brazen actor and Southern sympathizer. As the Lincoln funeral train took him home to Illinois, there were many stops for mourners.

Kennedy was 46, and Lincoln was 56 the Fridays they died.

Jacqueline Kennedy designed her husband's farewell with Lincolnesque echoes, such as a riderless horse. The world's heart broke.

Running for Congress, Lincoln opposed admitting Texas to the Union as a slave state. Even with Martin Luther King Jr. leading the civil rights movement and visiting the White House, Kennedy still felt he needed to win the huge Jim Crow Southern state for reelection in 1964.

That's why the president went to Dallas for that November noonday parade, despite warnings of danger.

We have Lincoln to thank for Thanksgiving, however far we are from loved ones this hard year. In 1863, the Civil War president proclaimed the New England custom a national holiday. It was a way to heal wounds and unify the people — across states, even at sea — with glimmers of gratitude for "fruitful land" and other gifts.

And a prayer for peace. Things were darkest then, but Lincoln saw some light.

Kennedy's 1963 Thanksgiving proclamation, just before his death, noted Lincoln's civic wisdom "in the midst of America's tragic civil war." He declared, "Our forefathers in Virginia and Massachusetts, far from home in a lonely wilderness, set aside a time of thanksgiving." The first was celebrated with Wampanoag indigenous people.

"The love that bound which bound them together" characterized the uniquely American rite, Kennedy wrote, urging us to share blessings and ideals widely across the world, pursuing "the great unfinished tasks of achieving peace, justice and understanding."

Bittersweet November, with roses in time's wind.

In Private Sieges, Missing Public Squares

Dec. 9, 2020

WASHINGTON—"We need each other." Bill Clinton once spoke those simple words. Never has that truth been truer than in the waning days of America's 2020. The year is truly Dickensian, with the pandemic changing everybody and everything in an uneven government response. The holidays will hurt many families, missing members.

People need to congregate in public spaces, not only churches and temples. People need to mix, cross paths by chance, catch one another's eyes and talk to pass the time. Children need to play. Young ones need to flirt and fall in love. Broadway actors need to perform before actual audiences. Doctors and teachers need to see their patients and pupils. "Remote learning" seems a cruel contradiction. Adults thrive on camaraderie as we go about daily rounds.

Zoom meetings and social media are ersatz and ethereal, thin gruel—like Oliver's porridge in the "Oliver Twist" orphanage.

On Dec. 7, we remember Pearl Harbor as a national bombshell. The 1941 milestone marked President Franklin D. Roosevelt's declaration of war, saying the attack was "a date which shall live in infamy." The president had a fully united nation with him upon entering World War II.

Hear me for this claim: In that world war, a spirited togetherness burned bright in both the war abroad and the mobilization at home. It was a good war, when the president had the ear of the people. It was a time you felt glad to be alive. My grandmother was a widowed nurse with four children who listened to Roosevelt's Fireside Chats to lift morale.

Always the cheery realist, Roosevelt was beloved and believed.

Now is not like then. After nine months, our lives feel like a siege, with a dispirited sense of apartness from enforced time at home. Private walls are closing in. California is under stay-at-home orders.

Once bustling, our shared public spaces are dry and clamped down by COVID-19, such as the human mosaic that used to enliven the Santa Monica Promenade. The grand Union Station here has a lonely great Christmas tree (a gift from Norway) standing in the center with nobody around it to sing, light or behold it. Few train travelers stream by toward the taxis waiting outside, in full view of the cold marble Capitol.

Stark sidewalks downtown have lost their step, the city ballet of walkers utterly absent. Buildings are nothing without the people. Think of all the conversations over coffees missed, the laughs, the ideas, the impulse store buys for the holidays. All the little losses can't be counted.

But you wouldn't believe how shabby Lafayette Square looks now, in front of the White House. It's barricaded, with signs left from the June street protests against police brutality. The square looks abandoned, an eyesore from any angle. The equestrian statue of President Andrew Jackson, who Trump says he admires, is obscured from public view.

This scene borders on criminal neglect of a historic square. Dolley Madison lived there. That was where women suffragists celebrated winning the vote in 1920.

We know Donald Trump left behind a wake of shambles and bleeding business bankruptcies. We didn't know he'd do much the same for the country and economy.

The ruined square speaks of revenge on elegance, public gatherings, a popular president, perhaps even on women. Staring, I couldn't shake the sensation that Trump has us — languishing with the fizz knocked out of life — pretty much where he wants us.

It's fair to say this president could not have done a better job of laying us low if he tried. He could not have cut the heart of democracy more cleanly. Contesting the "rigged" election isn't over yet.

Remember Abraham Lincoln spoke to the "better angels"

of our nature? Trump did the opposite, seeking darkness in our character. In Trump's world, bragging was the national pastime. We know his open racism, misogyny, xenophobia and lies seared our collective soul. He encouraged "us" to hate "them." Those scars won't heal so quickly.

On the winter solstice, Jupiter and Saturn will look like kissing cousins, a rare planetary event. As ancient people read the skies, this meant a calamity coming. For us, let's hope, it means one is going.

Life in a Dickensian-Trumpian Tale of Hard Times — at Christmas

Dec. 16, 2020

WASHINGTON — Monday was a pretty good day in the life of 2020.

Coronavirus vaccines began all over. The Electoral College sealed Joe Biden's presidential win, no blood spilled. Stirred by the pandemic, the Senate rose from slumber to help hardships visited upon us, considering a COVID-19 relief package.

Hallelujah chorus, anyone? The $748 billion to $908 billion is real money. The 16 senators who met in the middle vowed not to go home for the holidays until it's done and dusted.

On the date George Washington died in 1799, Dec. 14, American democracy lived to fight another day. We survived a siege on civil institutions — the census, post office and press — from *within*. All are constitutional.

To tell you the truth, bells aren't ringing. They are tolling in hearts for the 300,000 lives lost. Life still feels glum as we count the days to Christmas.

Washington feels much like living inside Charles Dickens' 1843 classic, "A Christmas Carol." Donald Trump, the hateful president, is our own Ebenezer Scrooge. Central casting.

Inescapable, greedy Ebenezer, the defiant sinner. "Hard and sharp as flint ... The cold within him froze his old features, nipped his pointed nose, shrivelled his cheek," Dickens wrote. "No wind that blew was bitterer than he."

The capital is a small town. You can't escape Trump's ugly temper here, the insults and lies he hurls every day into our square like a slugger's fastball. He gives new meaning to public dis-coarse.

There's a strange fascination with his brazenly breaking

every rule in the book—and all not written in the book.

The new White House casualty is crafty Attorney General William Barr, who resigned after serving Trump's purposes extremely well. He ordered tear gas attacks on peaceful protests in June. However, he didn't play his part in countless court challenges to election results, making Trump livid.

Barr also directed executions to go forward as maskless White House holiday parties raged.

For our tale, let Barr be like Scrooge's past partner, Jacob Marley. "Old Marley was as dead as a door nail," Dickens wrote.

Barr is just as dead to Trump, though he saved him from getting nailed by the Robert Mueller investigation report. But that was, like, so 2019, before the impeachment trial. Trump "won" by 51 Republican senators' silence and compliance.

That trial was the winter of 2020. If Trump hadn't spent his time beating the Ukraine rap, maybe he'd have done something about the global pandemic unfolding in February. Then again, maybe not.

The other day, 126 House Republicans shocked even world-weary us by signing on to Trump's last gasp in court. Amazing disgrace. They are no better than Trump's legion of Proud Boys, night rioters who vandalized two historically Black churches in Washington over the weekend.

Meanwhile, back at the Senate, a striking sight in the dark sky: Republicans and Democrats reaching consensus at the end of the dreary year. Seen in the same room.

"We're the only game in town," West Virginia Sen. Joe Manchin, a centrist Democrat, said. He led a bipartisan group to write a $908 billion emergency bill to take to congressional leaders and colleagues.

The legislation covers small business relief; rental, education and unemployment assistance; and aid for food programs and COVID-19 health care. It gives funding to the travel and public transportation sectors. Every penny of it is needed as a hard winter falls.

Passage depends on Senate Majority Leader Mitch McConnell, R-Ky., granting a vote and Trump's signature. The blue House will pass it.

Senators seemed jazzed to have the rare chance to do their job—legislating and compromising. That's the art of politics. But McConnell runs a tight floor, acting mostly on judges during a season of crisis.

Dickens came close to creating our Scrooge, but the bleak scale of the republic's 2020 suffering is writ large. Mankind was never the president's business: common welfare, charity, mercy, all that.

The grump-in-chief will dish out "Bah! Humbugs!" and coals and ashes as we count the time to high noon on Jan. 20. The worst is yet to come. For now, we have a minor miracle.

Said Virginia Democrat Mark Warner: "Sixteen senators came together. Let me enjoy the moment."

On a Long, Dark Night, Congress Caught Doing Something Right

Dec. 23, 2020

They say the personal is political. The political is also personal.

Spending hours under the Capitol dome as Congress negotiated a COVID-19 relief package, I saw personalities break through the hot air.

Sen. Cory Booker, D-N.J., literally walked in circles around the rotunda, carrying on a cellphone conversation among the statues.

That summed up the mood in the House and Senate chambers. Christmas was coming, with lawmakers stressed and pressed like you and me. Right up to the Monday midnight deadline, they passed an emergency $900 billion bill. At last.

Democratic Senate Minority Leader Charles Schumer called it a "shot in the arm," perhaps to link it to the new vaccine. He told me he "defanged" a late move to curb Federal Reserve emergency loans.

House Speaker Nancy Pelosi, D-Calif., who had a surprise up her bright red sleeve, declared, "Seven hundred hours from now, Joe Biden will be president." But who's counting?

The divided Congress result bodes well for Biden.

All agreed the legislation was way too late. Democrats felt it was too little aid for the suffering country in crisis, on the pandemic and economic fronts.

Still, it gave something for everyone. Republicans won tax breaks on corporate lunches. Democrats got assistance for renters, small businesses, food, child care and the jobless. Coronavirus testing and vaccines are buttressed. A direct payment of $600 to most adults is included.

Some showed more grace under pressure than others. A

bald Kansas Republican, Sen. Pat Roberts, sported a cowboy hat onto the formal Senate floor. A cattlemen's group gave it to Roberts, who is retiring, so heck, what does he care?

Senate Republican Leader Mitch McConnell, R-Ky., never broke from his calm, icy stare. He often passes reporters waiting by the Ohio grandfather clock without a word or clue of what he's going to do.

"Waiting for Mitch?" Sen. Sherrod Brown, an Ohio Democrat, asks us with a grin.

Josh Hawley, a freshman Republican senator with outsize confidence, told reporters, "If this is the best we can do, it's terrible, a mockery."

Hawley urged direct payments be higher as a stimulus but was loudly opposed by Sen. Ron Johnson, a wealthy Wisconsin Republican.

Sen. Tom Cotton, R-Ark., another young conservative, took a bitter verbal shot at the press gallery, which overlooks the floor. I was surprised, because I've seen the Senate in several phases and never witnessed that before.

That got me thinking about "giants of the Senate." Since before the Civil War, it was famed for speakers with a vision and gift for making laws and compromises to further the greater good.

I knew some as a rookie reporter, covering Sens. Edward Kennedy, Robert C. Byrd, Bob Dole, John McCain and other leaders respected across party lines. Their voices were listened to, especially Kennedy's hearty roar on the floor.

Byrd often touched on the Roman Senate, his compass. He told me the Roman Senate "ceded" its power to Julius Caesar. Caesar did not seize it. A lesson in presidential power.

Looking from the gallery, I spotted no Senate giants. A few could grow into giants, but they'd better hurry up, because the country needs some. South Dakotan Sen. John Thune, the Republican whip, is very tall, but no giant.

Sens. Dick Durbin, D-Ill., and Joe Manchin III, D-W.Va., chief builders of the bipartisan rescue package, said they saw more friendly spirit on the floor than all year. Working together lifts morale.

If any giant strides the Capitol's marble halls, it's Pelosi, a study in motion churning out statements and strategy. Her House is a host of progressive bills, compared with the Senate's stately pace under McConnell's thumb.

In a victory for history's court, the speaker just banished the statue of Confederate Gen. Robert E. Lee from the Capitol. For Christmas, the "noble" traitor is now gone from the house of the democracy he waged war against.

Thank you, Madam, nice gift.

Most of all, Pelosi had the courage to confront President Donald Trump all along, leading the way to his impeachment.

2020 began with the Senate impeachment trial and ran into the pandemic in mid-March.

The Senate approved the package's final passage on the winter solstice, 92-6.

Let's hope the darkest, longest night leads to January light.

Lord, What Did We Do To Deserve 2020?

Dec. 30, 2020

WASHINGTON—Just back from a sweet sight: President Donald Trump going out on a losing note with loyalists in Congress. The House voted to override a presidential veto—the one time it's happened in his one-term presidency. The House approved the $740 billion defense authorization bill over his objection, by a whopping 322-87 vote Monday. Even 109 stalwart House Republicans deserted Trump in his waning hours.

The Senate is likely to send the same rebuke, now stymied. The Republican leader, Mitch McConnell, R-Ky., is loath to hold a vote on the second big House bill Monday, which boosts COVID-19 relief payments to $2,000.

Senators, proud of the bipartisan defense bill, were annoyed at cutting their holiday short due to Trump's cavalier veto near Christmas. At year's end, political pressure will likely force the Senate to greenlight both bills. Note 130 House Republicans voted against higher direct payments—defying Trump's last stand.

What is the cure for what ails us?

Just look at a handful of headlines: "Millions of Jobless on brink of Poverty"; "Enduring the Final Days of Trump." Those are from USA Today. The Atlantic described "Our Broken Democracy." Mix in the deaths from the pandemic.

It's all over now, the pretense that we aren't ravaged, from seniors down to children crying because they miss school friends. Washington is exhausted on both sides, with reservoirs run dry by a vicious voice in tongue and tweet.

We're counting days until Jan. 20, President-elect Joe Biden's Inauguration Day. He projects sympathy—and solutions—for the discouraged and diminished.

Meanwhile, the losing one-term president is defying all the usual norms with his pardons. He has nothing and no friends left to lose. The country is hurting much more, laid low by the coronavirus and the fragile economy. If Trump's COVID-19 case was cured, then that's all he knows.

To the question: What did we to deserve the wrath of 2020?

In 1620, when the Mayflower pilgrims landed on Massachusetts shores, that question would be easy. Men could form aboard ship a pact of self-government. They might build a city on a hill and call it Boston. But things were really up to God.

In the 1740s, when we were colonies, Puritan preacher Jonathan Edwards gave a famous speech in Connecticut that made the bargain on earth clear, between God and us. We were "Sinners in the Hands of an Angry God," suffering and at the mercy of God. So, you better be good.

In 1820, we had the last known Era of Good Feelings in Washington. James Monroe, last in the "Virginian dynasty" presidents, was amiable. Things were sunny, but for the dark cloud of Southern slavery. Monroe owned slaves, fewer than the rest. But the institution was rapidly growing and created great wealth in the South. The Virginia planter presidents praised landed ways of life at the expense of thriving cities: cultural, shipping, banking and trading centers.

We were unifying as a nation, not just a bunch of states. I imagine President Monroe would put a cheery gloss on wearing masks and so on. People would have the plague embedded in memory, and Monroe might have appealed to that as well as their patriotism. A partisan divide over distancing and masks would not have frozen progress.

From 1918 to 1920, Woodrow Wilson was president during the global influenza epidemic. About 675,000 Americans died. Like Trump, Wilson shied away from taking it seriously, even after he was stricken by a secret illness, most likely influenza. He was negotiating a treaty in Paris with other world leaders (to end World War I). Wilson did not tell the American people he fell seriously ill. Some think he was never the same.

Wilson was the son of a Presbyterian minister. Was God displeased with his segregationist stance and opposition to women's suffrage for five years?

In our day, a secular democracy barely survived a stress test in peacetime. Still divided and sick, that's the price we pay for a rogue who was more pretender than president.

Among the politerati across America, Trump's wild-eyed words on the pandemic confirmed his dark character and caused much of the contagion.

We are the cure for what ails us.

Crisis

A Desperate Duel for Democracy

Jan. 6, 2021

Attention readers: Jamie Stiehm was in the press gallery of the House chamber when violence, breaking glass, shouts and tear gas broke out on Jan. 6.

WASHINGTON — Wednesday, the sixth day of the year, will be high drama, Shakespearean or Greek tragedy. During a massive joint session of Congress, there may be blood spilled on the streets after night falls here in the capital. The president invited, or incited, his violent Proud Boys to town. We are braced. Every police officer will be on duty.

The duel between President Donald Trump versus American democracy will be done. The two cannot coexist. Only one side shall live to tell how the other was vanquished.

The raving of a desperate man was revealed in a threatening call with a top Georgia state official who firmly told the ousted president he lost the red state.

The new Congress meets every four years for "certification" of the presidential election. The formality lasts an hour of good will. The vice president presides. Al Gore sat in that chair in 2001, after losing a 5-4 Supreme Court ruling to George W. Bush. He was good-natured, with rueful humor.

Certification is like the handshake after a tennis match, and other sporting rituals between victor and loser. Not anymore. It could take day and night.

Trump won't be in the room where the ritual happens. But his operatic outbursts will split the parties in a Capitol Grand Canyon, and even — and this is hard — drive a wedge between Republicans. After four years in office, Trump twisted the party to his will until the final hours, when some showed spirit.

But Trump's brazen quest to overturn the free and fair election is not over. It's as if the president declared war on American democracy. Tragically, he has accomplices, including an old Alabama football coach, Sen. Tommy Tuberville, R-Ala., a Senate freshman. No, I'm not making this up.

The Senate band in the parade was led by young, lean Sen. Josh Hawley, a Missouri Republican with a fancy Yale law degree. His vein of ambition shines and blares "2024." Republican Sen. Ted Cruz of Texas is another arrogant Ivy man trying to taint the 2020 election to win in 2024. Along with Wisconsin's Ron Johnson and other Republican senators, they bow and scrape to Trump's base.

Note: The "base" is now the mob, even those in expensive suits. A Proud Boys leader just got arrested for burning a Black Lives Matter banner from a historically Black church here on the 12th night of December. That night, in ugly street scenes, the pro-Trump hooligans wielded knives and Confederate flags.

Let's set the certification scene inside the Capitol, in the "People's House." Elegant Nancy Pelosi, D-Calif., was just reelected Speaker. The place will smolder with glee *and* angst as control of the Senate will be decided the night before in Georgia, of all places.

Either two Democratic challengers will win Senate seats or two Republican senators will hold their seats. Democrats Jon Ossoff and the Rev. Raphael Warnock ran a smart joint campaign against a pair of weak opponents and may paint Georgia and the Senate blue.

First, a goodly number of House Republicans planned to challenge state results. For a while, nobody cared because they needed senators to join the high-stakes scam. Senators think they're the classy chamber next to the boisterous House.

Senate Majority Leader Mitch McConnell, R-Ky., urged his caucus to stay out of this extraordinary caper. To his credit, I might add, for his loud chorus of critics.

McConnell is an expert on how the game is — and isn't — played. He gets bad press but plays by the rules and congratulated Joe Biden on winning. He's better than many Republican rotten apples in his caucus, about a baker's dozen, who vowed to disrupt certification.

What offends McConnell and me most: Four new freshmen senators signed onto this trouble, including the football coach. The clubby Senate likes freshmen to find the cloakroom before they rock riots.

Accepting the Speaker's gavel Sunday, Pelosi asked the House for peace, adding, "Let it begin with us." Moments later, irascible Republican Rep. Don Young of Alaska, the oldest House member, softened and spoke to the full floor: "We need to hold hands and talk to each other."

The duel between American democracy and Trump is upon us. One by day, the other by night.

'Capitolnacht': Darkness on the Nation's Doorstep

Jan. 13, 2021

America has our own "Capitolnacht." It shall cut and burn our conscience as Kristallnacht, the Night of Broken Glass, in Nazi Germany announced a civilized country's descent into dark evil and racial supremacy. Austrian-born Arnold Schwarzenegger compared the Nazis to the Proud Boys.

1938 history wouldn't happen here because we Americans have our heart in the right place as we pursue happiness, right? I was a history major who believed our rocky journey sailed in the right direction. Slavery, our tragic flaw, was past.

Then I witnessed the Capitol siege by white supremacists trying to overturn President Donald Trump's loss. I heard glass shatter in a rampage by a murderous mob. Thank God they were held at bay, barely. What a close call in the House of Representatives chamber, where hundreds gathered inside, including me and fellow journalists. Good Lord.

Unknown to us, the mob broke into the Senate chamber on the other side of the rotunda. One man brandished the ultimate hate symbol, a large Confederate flag within the walls and halls of the cherished Capitol. Wasn't that settled in 1865? Smelling salts, please.

On our House side, they were bloodthirsty for the speaker. Nancy Pelosi, the California Democrat, just kicked a Confederate Robert E. Lee statue out of the Capitol crypt for good. Worse, how dare a woman challenge Trump, time after time?

For those of us who thought the Civil War was over, think again. The bloody war was supposedly won by the Union. President Abraham Lincoln freed 4 million people in bondage. But the white supremacist South dressed up the romance of the "Lost Cause" and nurtured its hatred for generations. Melanie in "Gone With the Wind" vowed to teach her boy Beau to hate Yankees.

Trump embodies that embittered streak in Southern lore. His loss was a stolen victory to be avenged—just like the war that ended slavery. His racism is front and center, just like the Confederacy.

Most, not all, of the mob came from the South. The spirit of civil strife was the same that infused the antebellum South toward states north of the Mason Dixon line. The defiant senators who inflamed the election ritual, Sens. Josh Hawley, R-Mo., and Ted Cruz, R-Texas, come from former slave states.

What happened Wednesday did more than violate sacred space and spill blood in a riot. The rage of thousands—more organized than the Capitol police—revealed a campaign that cleaves the nation into "us and them" again, with only anger in the middle ground.

Trump, in effect, waged war on the United States government, just like Jefferson Davis, the Confederate president. Strikingly, each was a white supremacist who never surrendered. History rhymes.

Donald Trump and his family watched with grim glee as the house of American democracy was overtaken, ransacked and defaced. Inside the beloved Capitol, one heard the broken glass on marble floor first, followed by angry voices and gunshots outside the House chamber. Pelosi was presiding over the last official election ritual. Brave and poised, she was spirited away.

American pride in our democracy was breached by the mob violence as sure as walls and doors. Thousands were sent by Trump to terrorize Congress into changing the final count for the election, which he lost.

The Rev. Jesse Jackson, the civil rights leader, told me before the Women's March that Trump and his men were "Confederates." I spoke at a breakfast at the Woman's National Democratic Club and sat next to him. This was on Jan. 21, 2017.

Jackson was utterly serious. And he was utterly right. He's a native of South Carolina, where the South started the cannonballs flying160 years ago. Knowing the Civil War as well as I do, trapped in the siege as I was, it's clear we're in a civil war, small "c." The battle has begun for the best versus the worst in our body politic.

Liberals like me dismissed Trump as a buffoon or a toddler. We tolerated tirades that mixed racism, misogyny, "fake news" and "the radical left" as the president poisoned the public well.

And then he set the mob on us.

Racist Mobs Rage All Over American History

Jan. 20, 2021

WASHINGTON — Raging racist mobs hold a high place in American history. There I was, in the Capitol siege, with breaking glass, bloodthirsty shrieks and gunshots cascading down marble halls. The statues in democracy's house were weeping.

Inside the House chamber, there was no time to cry. We moved fast down a secret staircase to safety. Only later did we learn thousands came armed to the teeth and brought bear spray. Very nice. The hate left behind in shambles was head-spinning.

The Trump-led mob was loaded for more than bear. They flew many miles to overthrow the presidential election by force. There's a first time for everything.

Make no mistake, there was a mob on the inside of the Capitol, too, dressed in suits and ties. There were 139 House Republicans who were part of the plot to undo democracy, led by two slick senators, Ted Cruz, R-Texas, and Josh Hawley, R-Mo. They give the Ivy League a bad name. They weren't wearing horns and helmets, but Hawley signaled his support to the outdoor mob. Looking spiffy, Republicans kept up their hated challenge after the siege.

The scale was stunning. The crowd comes from the darkest river in our history. White supremacists flourished under President Donald Trump, who has been watering their hatred like a garden since the Charlottesville, Virginia, deadly riot in his first summer.

The connection from Charlottesville back to the Ku Klux Klan is right in plain sight. Two Confederate general statues were the life of the party in downtown Charlottesville. (I don't even want to say their names.) The rioters showed up in force to "defend" the two traitors.

The Ku Klux Klan began in 1865 with embittered former

Confederate Gen. Nathan Bedford Forrest, known for his murderous ways. The Klan gave a way for "respectable" white Southern men to meet at night, put on hoods and terrorize Black men. Lynchings went on in the former slave states, even Maryland, into the 20th century.

The Klan aimed to enforce white supremacy, hold Black communities hostage to fear and undo the Civil War's meaning. The death toll is only now being honored, in Alabama's National Lynching Memorial.

The first Civil War blood was spilled in Baltimore, when a mob attacked Union soldiers.

It's even worse than that if you're obsessed with abolitionists, like me. Oh, how mobs hated the abolitionist movement, founded in Philadelphia in 1833.

The 1830s were paradise for racist mobs. Paradise. As far north as Boston, William Lloyd Garrison was nearly lynched, saved by the skin of his teeth. He founded the American Anti-Slavery Society. That set the tone for the violence that stalked abolitionists all over antebellum America. They were braver than we are.

Southern slaveowner Andrew Jackson was president during the dark lawless 1830s, nicknamed "King Mob." He's Trump's favorite.

In Philadelphia, the Quaker City, a racist Southern mob burned down a brand-new temple for anti-slavery gatherings. The mayor surrendered, saying his small police force couldn't defend the beautiful building. 1838, meet 2021.

Then the mob (medical students) rampaged through the streets and destroyed a "colored" orphanage. They almost burned down the house of Quaker heroine, Lucretia Mott, a leading abolitionist voice which rang like the bell of freedom.

Read on to the first martyr for the First Amendment. Elijah Lovejoy, an abolitionist editor, was often threatened by the mayor, the doctor, the "good people" of Alton, Illinois, to cease his radical press.

Lovejoy refused. Small-town citizens murdered Lovejoy

and threw his printing press in the Mississippi River. The slave state of Missouri, Hawley's state, is on the other side. 1837 led to 2021, too.

As former Sen. Paul Simon wrote, the people who really killed Lovejoy were "the middle of the road straddlers ... too timid to stand and be counted."

I've taken stands alone against a racist Cub Scout in second grade; an anti-gay effigy by a fraternity; and a Senate staff that shunned me for something my brilliant author boyfriend, Michael Lewis, wrote about Sen. Joe Lieberman. Not all mobs carry pitchforks.

Nonviolent struggle against mob fury is a hard road to hoe, as Quakers and the Rev. Martin Luther King Jr. found. But the discipline is the best way to take to lasting peace.

The Mob Cannot Go Home Again

Jan. 27, 2021

WASHINGTON — Peaceful democracy won and beat back the mob that stormed the Capitol on Jan. 6. But it was a close call. I know, having been there, inside the House chamber, when glass was broken and shots were fired. The raging shrieks of the mob still wake me.

As the duke of Wellington said, looking back at England's magnificent victory over Napoleon in the 1815 Battle of Waterloo, "the nearest-run thing you ever saw in your life."

I know just what he means. The armed, organized mob nearly won the day against civilians, lawmakers and a police force that lost control of the building.

Two weeks after thousands stormed the Capitol, we witnessed a sane, somber transfer of power in the heart of our capital city, heavily guarded as if in a war zone. The new president, Joe Biden, won a civilian victory every bit as important as Waterloo. He returned us to our senses and moved many to tears at his inaugural's reminder of the usual American norms, decency and other things we used to take for granted.

We should remember that close call and be more vigilant, friends and citizens. The second Senate impeachment trial of former President Donald Trump gives American democracy a chance to shut him out, silence him and lock him down. This is the man who emboldened the darkest sides of our country's character.

If the Senate acts properly in punishing Trump for inciting the insurrection, he can never run for office again. He is already banned from mainstream social media, the way he built his violent political following. That's a start in shunning him, banishing him from the realm, even if he's a free man in Mar-a-Lago. We may all play a part in this.

But first, let me tell you that the Capitol siege could so

easily have ended in much more blood spilled on the beautiful marble floors. In a matter of mere moments and split seconds, lawmakers, especially senators, narrowly escaped to safety.

The Proud Boys and Oath Keepers were among the marauders who came to undo the presidential election with baseball bats, plastic handcuffs and — come on — bear spray. Did the mob really intend to hang Vice President Mike Pence, presiding on the Senate side? What was the makeshift gallows for?

A disturbing number of those charged, about 1 in 5, have military training. They knew how to handle weapons. A crying shame that was not heard in the tumult: that the lighthouse of democracy, built largely by enslaved people, was vandalized by white supremacists.

Those shattering images can't be gone from our collective mind in a couple of weeks. The calls for "normalcy" fall flat. Our weakened system, after the assault, is akin to a patient that, like me, needs time to heal.

Rep. Jason Crow, D-Colo., says that business as usual can't go on: "Those who turned their backs on democracy under Trump will do it again if given the chance." A former Army Ranger, he decided to fight the mob with a pen if they broke into the House chamber.

As for us civilians in the public square, it's time to admit what passes for discourse is more like "discoarse." How social is "social media" at the end of the day? How much poison and hate talk can we tolerate?

"Fox News" is an oxymoron. Rush Limbaugh abuses free speech with the most vicious tongue in show business.

The violent mob did not come from the air, tweets and the ether — until, yes, it did. The internet connected thousands from hither and yon. Ready to be radicalized, they acted on a call to arms by a rogue president that lost the popular vote, twice.

The FBI has charged hundreds, which means that thousands are still at large.

So many people are turning in friends and family members who took part in the Capitol riot. These acts of courage should be thanked. They're not letting business as usual go on. The public must pressure the Senate to convict Trump.

Polite American society has to shame supporting Trump.

In years to come, nobody will want to tell their grandchildren they stormed the Capitol.

Profiles in Cowardice: The Mob Still Haunts the Halls

Feb. 3, 2021

The mob's shrieks in the Capitol siege stay with me. That's where the Republican Party is now, at their mercy. The mob roams the building still, at the heart of our plagued democracy.

Republicans in Congress who aided and abetted the outrage are profiles in cowardice. That makes 150 of them, but we'll single out the prize-winners. They dress in red ties and suits, mostly, and look clean-cut. But they answer to the same master as the mob.

Rep. Kevin McCarthy, R-Calif., and Sen. Mitch McConnell, R-Ky., House and Senate Republican leaders, pandered to former President Donald Trump for years. Little did they mind his hate talk and lawless schemes. McConnell merrily stocked the federal judiciary like a fishpond. Jocular McCarthy loved being in the fraternity surrounding the president.

Since I witnessed the Capitol crime scene, it's clear McConnell and McCarthy were appalled—at first—by the violent tens of thousands sent by Trump to overturn the election. They each laid the blame at his door.

"The mob was fed lies. They were provoked by the president," McConnell said in a rare moment of truth. He had taken six weeks to say Joe Biden won the 2020 election.

For once, the leaders stood up to the ogre in the Oval.

Then a sea change: Republican righteous indignation faded in the mists of a bleak midwinter.

McConnell and McCarthy could have led principled opposition to Trump in their caucuses. They failed at a perilous point in American democracy. Spectacularly.

They are prize-winning profiles in cowardice forever in history. The sound of their silence is deafening. McCarthy proved the most craven coward of all, going to Mar-a-Lago to appease Trump.

What does McCarthy have to fear? Going back to Bakersfield, California, his hometown? Or the hostile freshman Rep. Marjorie Taylor Greene, R-QAnon-Ga., threatening the House at the barrel of a gun?

At the least, McCarthy should defend decency by removing the raving Trump defender from her committees before Democrats do. Even McConnell denounced her "loony lies" as a "cancer" on the party.

As for McConnell, he could have atoned by reaching out to retiring Sens. Rob Portman, R-Ohio, Patrick Toomey, R-Pa., and Richard Burr, R-N.C., to start building a coalition of 17 Republican senators to seal conviction in Trump's upcoming trial. Fifty Democrats need 67 votes to convict Trump.

In the ransacked Capitol, Burr declared Trump "bears responsibility by promoting the unfounded conspiracy theories."

Senate Republicans Mitt Romney of Utah, Lisa Murkowski of Alaska and Ben Sasse of Nebraska may have joined that coalition.

But Trump, some say, "built the party back up" out of the wilderness. He cuts a fearsome figure. Out of office, impeached twice and facing a Senate trial next week, he still inspires fear from Republicans, who quail at his tweets of wrath.

Fear not. The Don tweets no more. The man in Mar-a-Lago exile can't evict 10 House Republicans who voted to impeach, but he'll try. Oh, he's fuming at the woman who dared defy him, Rep. Liz Cheney, R-Wyo. She gets a little red badge of courage.

Actually, Trump led the Republican party *into* the wilderness. They lost the White House, the Senate and the House under his watch. They no longer govern the country, save for the Supreme Court stranglehold.

In electoral politics, Trump lost the popular vote twice. After inciting the insurrection — and the impeachment charge —

polls suggest most Americans see him as a scourge.

Republican leaders admit outgoing Trump helped the party lose the two Georgia Senate seats that decided control of the Senate. The runoff was on Jan. 5, the day before the mob stormed the Capitol.

McConnell hates Trump for the scoundrel he is. He tried to avoid the incendiary Republican challenge to the Electoral College count on Jan. 6. He's not a leader of the mob. McCarthy is leading the well-dressed one.

In the brash young guard of Senate Republicans, Ivy Leaguers Josh Hawley, R-Mo., and Ted Cruz, R-Texas, played to the Trump riot by challenging the election count. Along with Rand Paul, R-Ky., and Tom Cotton, R-Ark., they're Southern sour without the charm. The four make McConnell's lack of moral courage seem like a warmup act.

Brace for more storms coming.

The Capitol Trial on the President's Riot

Feb. 10, 2021

The second impeachment trial of former President Donald John Trump opened Tuesday afternoon. It's the Super Bowl of all impeachments, with a single charge: The president incited an insurrection against Congress to overturn the 2020 election. Nothing like it has ever happened in our American story.

The House managers made an earthshaking case yesterday on the Jan. 6 Capitol riot.

So, I have news for other journalists.

It's not for us to write, tell or tweet the conventional wisdom that 50 Democratic senators won't win the 17 Republican votes needed to convict Trump. We like to act as if we know it all ahead of time.

"Very unlikely," opined Peter Alexander, an NBC News correspondent who doesn't even cover Congress.

In this national drama, it's unfair to the public not to play it as it lays. Let the process play out, just as the Super Bowl game did. Let the battle be lost or won as the trial unfolds. Otherwise, we detract from engaging with the trial's grave meaning.

The power of press influence is a real factor on the field.

We in the world-weary media could affect the outcome, in a weird Washington way. Let's not let the 50 Republican senators off the hook by assuming their votes are good as gone.

The result *should* be unclear at this point. Some Republican senators may vote their conscience, which is what the public expects.

Mitch McConnell, the Senate Republican leader from Kentucky, can't stand Trump, and he's not the only one. Sen. Rand Paul, R-Ky., who contends they can't impeach a leader who's left office, won support for that notion. But he's one of the least liked senators.

In the hurly-burly of an impeachment trial and public

opinion, senators will be watching one another carefully. They will listen to constituents. There will be room for political mercury, surprises and tipping points.

And a handful may feel guilt at what their party hath wrought.

In February 1999, senators could not vote to convict President Bill Clinton over a slight affair. Public opinion sided with a president in peace and prosperity.

Looming large in the Senate chamber are haunting memories of fleeing an armed mob ready to take no prisoners. The Senate's dignity was taunted, defiled, ransacked. Some rioter with horns and fur, a QAnon "shaman," outrageously sat in the vice president's chair.

Mike Pence was presiding over the constitutional ritual of confirming the Electoral College count. The mob had a gallows for him, Trump's greatest loyalist.

The spectacle was outlandish and tragic. In the House chamber, where I was, we heard gunshot right outside the ornate speaker's lobby. The Capitol felt like a war zone, even to combat veterans. The 100 senators, trial jurors, were witnesses to the crime scene.

The House managers, headed by Rep. Jamie Raskin, D-Md., will connect dots and present video images showing the raucous crowd taking directions from Trump by the White House to the murderous march to the Capitol.

When they arrived, the mob was in a frenzy. Rioters injured 139 police officers as they rammed windows and fought their way into the building. Many had military training to use against civilians — not a peaceful assembly covered by the First Amendment.

The world witnessed the armed mob storm the Capitol, following Trump's orders, "We fight like hell," in a rally. The violence tens of thousands did to the burnished halls, rooms and doors can be repaired.

For those like me inside the siege, memories of bloodthirsty shrieks, broken glass, pounding footsteps and white supremacist flags stay with you. Blood fell on marble floors. Statues wept.

And it could have been so much worse.

In 1868, the dour white supremacist President Andrew Johnson came in one vote shy of conviction in his impeachment trial. Like Trump, he never won a popular vote. He's like Trump's history cousin, only better.

I remember Trump's first trial seen from the press gallery, clear as a February day in 2020. There was one lone "guilty" vote from the Republican side: the urbane Utahn, Sen. Mitt Romney.

Then Trump was charged with interfering with the election using a foreign power, Ukraine.

Now we see that as child's play, next to inciting an insurrection. Child's play.

Painting Parallels of Presidents' Civil Wars

Feb. 17, 2021

WASHINGTON — Some Presidents Day: icy with a bitter blow in the wind.

I'm telling myself the impeachment trial vote on former President Donald Trump was a moral victory. The Senate tally was 57 guilty, 43 not guilty. Seven Republicans joined 50 Democrats for a 14-vote margin. That's a rebuke for the Jan. 6 deadly riot he caused at the Capitol.

Yet it came up short of conviction, which requires 67 votes, two-thirds of the body. The House managers, full of vim and vigor, could not have moved one more sullen Republican senator.

The tragedy was the war within the Republican leader. Senate Minority Leader Mitch McConnell, R-Ky., clearly dearly wished to have the courage to vote against Trump, but yielded to his partisan self. He could have made all the difference.

I witnessed the drama with my own eyes, from the Senate press gallery. The face of Republican Senator Richard Burr of North Carolina reddened with anger when scenes of the attack on the Capitol were played. I suspected he'd diverge and vote "guilty," which he did.

That very chamber was invaded by white men with helmets and horns. The quaint 19th-century desks were ransacked. Confederate flags waved outside the floor.

The angry mob called for the vice president's neck as he presided over the Electoral College count that afternoon. Trump called a freshman senator to see what was going on after the violence started, as if he didn't know.

Mike Pence barely escaped with his life, as the trial showed, just steps and moments from the marauders.

One lawyer for Trump, Michael van der Veen, was just as mean-spirited and mendacious as his client. Trump knows how to pick them.

We know an American president never before seized the Capitol by murderous force to overturn an election he has lost. That makes Trump the worst president ever.

What we don't know is that it will never happen again. There's the rub: 43 Republican senators chose not to punish the former president, who will take that as a license to further destabilize and divide our democracy.

When I went to the Capitol, it was my first time back since Jan. 6. I was in the House chamber press section when we heard breaking glass, shrieks and gunshots right outside the doors. Suddenly, we were in a siege, day and night, started while democracy's work was being done.

Going back, I walked across an eerily empty National Mall, toward the marble-domed citadel, which had a massive iron fence a mile around it. I had to circle around a square Brutalist building. Sharp-shooting soldiers were stationed at every block and told me to keep my press pass visible.

Such is the shambles of a peaceful democracy, a torn, ragged legacy for President Joe Biden.

I thanked the Capitol police I saw "for everything" when I finally entered. We were lucky; it was a close call on both sides. The House managers told us the mob meant to kill House Speaker Nancy Pelosi, D-Calif., spirited out in the nick of time.

Back at the beloved Capitol, the spirit was not the same. Distrust, division and sadness cut the air. As we pick up pieces of an uncivil war raging in the temple of democracy, the anger is rising like bread.

Pelosi condemned the "cowardly group of (43) Republicans ... maybe they can't get another job."

By contrast, Abraham Lincoln was our greatest president. My mind flew to him, riding the train bound for Washington in another bleak February, soon to be sworn in March 4, 1861. An unknown from Illinois, he arrived in a sharp, tense, divided capital city of a country already breaking apart.

Along the way, he survived a murder plot in Baltimore. Several Southern slave states seceded before his inaugural. We were on the cusp of the Civil War, declared by the Confederacy. Lincoln didn't start fights, but he never lost any.

Lincoln left Springfield, Illinois, on Feb. 11, just before his 52nd birthday. At the parting, he told townspeople at the train station, "I now leave, not knowing when, or whether ever, I may return."

He saved the Union and ended slavery. But Lincoln never returned home, the Civil War's final casualty.

Let's not do it over again.

Biden Knows His Task:
To Repair Broken Parts and Hearts

Feb. 24, 2021

WASHINGTON—Picture America as a big house in Texas.

The place seems wrecked, along with the people in it. They are stranded without power, light, water—after a gale force.

They fear it's beyond repair and are losing faith in the future. The parents wonder how they're going to pay their bills with lost jobs. The children want to go to school and see friends they miss.

We are all Texans now, with Texas the outsize canvas of misery after severe winter storms.

Joe Biden's presidency is only a month old, but the mission is clear: to heal and repair America's hurting hearts, homes, hopes and health. His talent for empathy matches the moment of this urgent task. He knows this town well and never met a stranger.

The four years of Donald Trump's presidency left a wake of despair, death, tax breaks for the rich, racism, cruelty and a Capitol riot. Deadly violence under the dome was the tragedy's final act.

Enter Biden. He brings a ray of reassurance that our house can be fixed to stand strong again. Biden's presidency may go down as the trusty Repairman Era.

Unlike former President Barack Obama, Biden does not bring beautiful words to the table. That's fine; it's no problem to talk low-tempo like genial Joe. If he gets things done, who needs fancy solos in a state of crisis?

In fact, the sound of silence falls sweetly here after all the noise and tweets Trump trumpeted. Friends said how moving Biden's simple, somber words were during a South Portico candlelight ceremony for COVID-19 losses—personal yet addressed to all. The president spoke after a moment of silence on remembrance and healing.

"I know all too well," Biden said. "The survivors' remorse, the anger, the questions of faith in your soul."

Many Americans already call him Joe.

A Washington denizen, he knows what the law can do, how presidents can help real people in their real lives, as he sends federal disaster assistance and plans to visit Texas, the beleaguered Lone Star State.

Biden, 78, is now the best version of himself, a work in progress for years. His kind temperament and tone matter greatly to a country or family feeling abused and abandoned. We are collectively clinging to the wreckage, in a British author's phrase.

Let's go over the three most important fronts.

Climate change is of the essence. The polar vortex storms in Texas, forest fires in California, rising sea levels and melting glaciers are all connected. Biden immediately rejoined the Paris Agreement, to our allies' delight. Trump had dropped out of this landmark treaty on climate goals.

The COVID-19 pandemic just reached a grave milestone of 500,000 deaths in one year. Biden signaled from the start that the nation would honor the dead and buttress the living with a mass public health program combining masks ("for God's sake"), social distancing and vaccinations reaching 100 million this spring.

This sound medical strategy contrasts with Trump's almost criminal carelessness about the death toll and protecting the populace.

As his wife Melania put it on a shirt: "I really don't care. Do U?" That was Trump's stance on the coronavirus, which he knew was highly contagious.

The battered economy needs love and money. A nearly $2 trillion package is almost out the door. The House is set to approve the American Rescue Plan this week.

Biden courted Senate Republican support, but says he'll

sign the bill without a Republican vote. That's good-will politics, to hold out a hand to the other side, true blue to one's own party.

Cabinet appointments show that Biden values expertise, after being around the block a time or two. In poetic justice, Merrick Garland is set to be attorney general after Obama let him languish as a Supreme Court nominee.

Garland, Treasury Secretary Janet Yellen and other Cabinet members telegraph they will work for the American people, not cater to the president's ego.

"I'm not the president's lawyer," Garland stated in a Senate hearing. He called the Capitol riot "heinous" and said investigating the mob attack is first on his list.

To repair the broken parts — Biden and his team have the right stuff. Refreshing.

Don't Fence the Capitol In or Out

March 3, 2021

WASHINGTON — Two women are deciding paths of our destiny, the acting Capitol police chief and the Senate parliamentarian. You and I — and the lamppost — don't know them.

One unknown gave us something deeply wrong; the other took away something deeply right. Strange for strangers to have such untold, unelected power in a democracy, while we pick up pieces from shambles.

Happy Women's History Month, everybody.

We've never seen anything like the massive fence imprisoning the Capitol after the Jan. 6 riot — a terrible message for the temple of democracy. Razor wire and soldier sharpshooters all around the dome for a country mile. The landscape looks like martial law. Sen. Richard Burr, R-N.C., told me, "I wish they'd tear the thing down." It's former President Donald Trump's parting gift, his writing on our National Mall. He sent legions of white supremacists marching to "fight like hell."

But the military overkill is due to the acting Capitol police chief, Yogananda Pittman. Her boss, Steven Sund, got fired on Jan. 7. She's a scaremonger but has not taken responsibility for her police force losing control of the Capitol to the armed mob.

I was there that day, in the siege. The mob was better organized. There were heartbreaking police casualties and heroics. But the chief leaders were unprepared, despite an FBI warning.

Meanwhile, something happened inside the dome contrary to the currents of most lawmakers and citizens.

The Senate parliamentarian threw out raising the minimum wage to $15 in the pending American Rescue Plan. Just like that. One woman, one vote.

This raise for working Americans, meant to lift families out of poverty, was part of the COVID-19 stimulus package passed by the House. Now its heart languishes on a deathbed in the Senate.

Meet Elizabeth MacDonough, the obscure parliamentarian. Who knew she was the keeper of the keys? The mob ransacked her book-lined Capitol office, where she dwells, quiet as a mouse.

Does the parliamentarian care to live on $7.25 hourly, the federal minimum wage? Let her try.

The nearly $2 trillion package was written for the country's crisis in quiet desperation. The pandemic and economic fronts are related. They rise or fall together. History calls for bold, sweeping action, following in the shoes of the New Deal during the Depression.

Sen. Bernie Sanders, I-Vt., voiced disbelief. "I regard it as absurd that the parliamentarian, a Senate staffer elected by no one, can prevent a wage increase for 32 million workers."

There's no time for technicalities. Sanders has a point, and he's not alone.

The man from Vermont vows to start a campaign to "ignore" or overrule the parliamentarian. House Speaker Nancy Pelosi, D-Calif., is impatient with the Senate's glacial speed even now, a year into the pandemic.

The "Byrd rule" is how MacDonough justified her decision that raising the minimum wage was "extraneous." The late Robert C. Byrd, a West Virginia Democrat, might not mind. I knew him well, a brilliant statesman from a poor state. Raised by a coal miner, Byrd knew in his marrow that government could make all the difference in rocky times.

Years ago, Byrd joined Sen. Edward Kennedy in championing a higher minimum wage.

President Joe Biden loves the Senate labyrinth. He'll let MacDonough's decision remain undisturbed.

Back to Pittman, a deputy chief thrust in the glare of a deadly debacle. She sounded a vague alarm of a plot to blow up the Capitol when Biden addresses Congress — not supported by the FBI.

Much of the Capitol gardens and terrace has been taken away from the public since I was a rookie reporter for The Hill and roamed freely. When it snows, children used to sled on the hill the Capitol crowns.

Frederick Law Olmsted, the genius who designed Central Park, created the inviting west front staircase that connects to the Mall. Since Sept. 11, the complex is scarred by bollards and checkpoints — none of which would keep a plane from crashing into the marble citadel.

The Capitol lantern lights the world — once upon a time, not long ago. Pittman now wants a more permanent fence with razor wire, with a smaller footprint.

Neither Pittman nor the parliamentarian seem to see the larger vision of what the Capitol stands for.

We need women of the people.

Democrats Seize the Spring and March With More Spirit

March 24, 2021

WASHINGTON — Under the spring sun, something stirs. After a withering four-year winter, Democrats are dancing with the daffodils.

Days are longer and hearts are lighter on Pennsylvania Avenue, from the White House to the Capitol.

Now in power, Democrats are getting radicalized, in a good way. The nearly $2 trillion COVID-19 and stimulus bill, signed by President Joe Biden, was larger and more liberal than some dared hope. Now Biden has a $3 trillion infrastructure package in the works.

The turn in the wind is real. It's blowing anew in the season of hope and crossing over to freedom.

On Capitol Hill, Democrats are not trying to work with Republicans anymore after a bloody riot and two presidential impeachments. Especially in the House, Democrats look upon the 139 Republicans who aided the riot with distrust and disgust.

After the Jan. 6 Capitol siege by a pro-Trump mob, democracy can't be business as usual. Not after vicious violence that ended with a police officer dead and 140 casualties.

Winters framed the pandemic, which made life stark and plain. What counts, and who matters. Your friends and enemies are like yes and no. Simple as that. In the face of loss, we are all changed and sobered. Frills melt away.

That urgency is real in the People's House.

The Democratic majority is marching forward, passing bills to contain the American tragedy of gun violence in Boulder, Colorado, and Atlanta, Georgia, and expand the Affordable Care Act. They passed a sweeping voting rights bill, the For the People Act. They voted to restore legal status to the "Dreamers" who came to the country as children.

In a slap, the House repealed the Muslim travel ban, President Donald Trump's first act in office. Statehood for the District of Columbia — Washington has 700,000 residents — has a heartbeat.

House Democrats — with many women in white to honor the suffrage struggle — are taking steps to ratify the Equal Rights Amendment. The Violence Against Women Act is not far behind. The Equality Act for LGBTQ Americans was approved to send to the Senate.

Truth be told, Democratic caucus members must sprint to keep up with the energized House Speaker, Nancy Pelosi, who turns 81 on Friday. (Happy birthday, Madam Speaker). The California Democrat is the only woman in history to hold the top post.

Just days ago, Pelosi rose to speak on the Dreamers. "This issue is near and dear to my heart," she declared. "Three years ago, I came to the floor and spoke about our Dreamers for eight hours and six minutes."

Indeed, Pelosi did, when the House was red with foot soldiers to Trump. Growing up as the daughter of the Baltimore mayor, she brings the same bold spirit to the work in the minority or majority. She was radicalized against Trump all along.

The Speaker led the resistance to the former president, in private and public, during the long Trump winter. From the get-go, when he crowed he won the popular vote, she corrected him in person. He hated that.

Last June, Pelosi said to Trump's face, "All roads lead to Putin." She was the only woman at the White House table.

The best stand-up moment was when Pelosi ripped up Trump's speech right there on the dais after his State of the Union speech.

Nonviolent resistance trumps the mob.

How refreshing to see team spirit cross over to both chambers. Winning does wonders for morale.

Now, for the first time, Senate Majority Leader Charles

Schumer, D-N.Y., and Pelosi drive the trains in the Capitol.

Yes, from New York to San Francisco, East and West Coasts. We're not in Kansas anymore—or Kentucky, the home of Senate Republican Leader Mitch McConnell.

But the Senate could be mistaken for the slow boat to China. Democrats are weighing getting rid of the filibuster—a radical move—meaning that bills could pass by a majority vote. The Senate needs to stay in step with the House and the times.

As it is, nearly all bills require 60 votes to pass because of the filibuster. Senators are so evenly divided they can't get 60 to agree on anything. With Biden's blessing, that vestige may soon be let go.

Then Democrats may tiptoe through the tulips.

The Plagues of Democracy — God Help Us

May 26, 2021

WASHINGTON — First, the plague shadowed the land. Then came the siege. Now locusts are swarming everywhere from the Capitol to the National Cathedral.

Let us pray. Lord have mercy on us, living in biblical times.

What's next, Exodus?

The coronavirus claimed more than half a million lives. It made us hold on to one another tighter, at a social distance. The Fourth of July never looked so good for a family reunion.

COVID-19 sobered and changed Americans of all ages and kinds. Never in memory have we faced collective loss, suffering that spares nobody.

Few could foresee America brought to its knees by a plague.

Meanwhile, the locusts — or cicadas — are breaking, as we speak, out of the ground into trees and sidewalks all over the East Coast.

By the trillions, they visit us every 17 years. Sure enough, they're crawling and crunching right on time in spring 2021.

Harmless, they say. Of course, our verdant Washington is the epicenter of the entire buzzing locust swarm. Our nerves can't take much more.

I met my first little locust on the House side of the Capitol as I prepared to enter the building. It had telltale red eyes. Yes, red eyes. Not much surprises me anymore.

Soon, they'll sing us to sleep at night.

The House of Representatives chamber is where I was on Jan. 6 for a great seat at the Capitol siege.

Up in the press gallery, overlooking Congress counting the presidential vote, we heard gunshots under us in the Speaker's Lobby. The howl of the mob was not to be forgotten. They didn't even sound human.

One Southern Democrat bellowed at the Republicans:

"This is because of you!"

All we in the press and the politicians knew was that the rotunda was breached—which was unthinkable. Steps away.

We heard the terrible sound of glass breaking in the marble halls. Within moments, the mob who stormed the Capitol tried to storm the chamber, where hundreds of us held our breath.

The closest call I ever hope to see.

It wasn't Masada, the Judaean fortress where Israelites died by suicide under siege by Roman soldiers. I've seen that sacred space.

But we were besieged. The danger of an armed mob was real enough, marauding though the sacred sanctum of democracy.

Americans saw just how vulnerable our way of life was, under attack from within. The bloodthirsty mob was incited in plain air by the then-president.

They brutally injured 140 Capitol and Metropolitan police for hours, with makeshift weapons. Some wore helmets and horns. The violence was astounding. The Pentagon was hours late to the game, perhaps on purpose.

Senators escaped in split-second timing before the mob charged into their chamber. They were thousands strong, some former military members.

The rest of us rushed down a secret staircase. We were under lockdown for hours.

Leaders of Congress and Vice President Mike Pence were brave and determined to return to finish the Electoral College count.

That's the best thing to say about the dark day's descent into night.

Yet nearly 150 Republican lawmakers kept up their challenge to state counts, despite the tragedy we just witnessed.

Bad blood got worse.

The count was done at 4 a.m. by the Senate's Ohio Clock.

Democracy lived to see another day. Joe Biden was officially the next president.

Lord, why did the siege happen here when it never happened before in American history?

God was mad at us for letting the former president act like an Egyptian pharaoh. Or a Roman emperor.

Yes, that makes sense.

Here is how Exodus records Moses and the locusts:

"And the locusts went up over the land of Egypt ... they covered the face of the whole earth, so that the land was darkened; and they did eat every herb ... and all the fruits."

Pioneers faced such a plague.

Author Laura Ingalls Wilder describes a cloud of grasshoppers hailing on her prairie family, eating away at their corn, potatoes, beans and Pa's wheat.

"Not a green thing was in sight anywhere."

Hopefully cicadas won't devour our city. We swear to do better as a free people, by God. No floods, OK?

Actually, it's raining pretty hard.

A Love Lost: The Senate and Me

June 2, 2021

WASHINGTON — I loved the Senate once — I thought for good — until midnight Friday.

Hours later, Senate Republicans failed America by blocking a bipartisan commission to get at the truth of the Jan. 6 storming of the Capitol.

The House already gave its blessing to a blueprint like the 9/11 Commission, with 35 Republican votes.

The blame was all the Senate's, the clubby "upper chamber."

Walking there in the noonday sun, I was ready to stay all day. As a witness to the deadly winter siege, I had to show faith in the arc bending toward justice.

But the Senate seemed like a stuck ship. Hours passed on the Ohio Clock.

With nothing going on, no planes to catch, senators and journalists had more time to talk. We let our hair down and took our masks off for the first time.

Glad I saved a chicken salad sandwich from the basement carryout.

Joe Manchin, a centrist Democrat from West Virginia, scolded all opposing the bill, saying the House gave Republicans an equal say in setting up the commission.

An Ohio senator told me on the elevator the Jan. 6 bill wasn't going to pass.

What did he know? I still had hope for a Hollywood ending in Washington.

For example, I saw Officer Eugene Goodman, the valiant police officer who diverted the mob in the wrong direction. Standing sentry by the Senate door, he was keeping senators safe — again.

Members of the Senate had a close call, running down an antique staircase, escaping the mob's fury with seconds to spare.

Over in the House chamber, we heard gunshots, breaking glass and howls that didn't sound human.

There were thousands, wielding weapons, injuring 140 police officers who defended us from harm. They scaled the walls of the temple.

A Republican woman's words rang true: The truth was hard stuff.

"An independent commission can provide answers we need," Lisa Murkowski, the senior Alaska senator, told a scrum of reporters. "There's more to be learned."

Or, she asked, "Is everything just one election after another?"

She fit my storyline. The 50 Democrats only needed nine more Republicans like her to win the showdown.

Then a chilling thought in the press gallery: The Trumpian mob picked up where the 9/11 hijackers left off. The plane to hit the Capitol was thwarted, 20 minutes away in the turquoise sky.

Of course, we know the Capitol was the intended target of the doomed plane that passengers took down — *thanks to the 9/11 Commission report.*

So, the stage was set, but the players — the 100 senators — were mostly off-stage and strangely muted in speeches.

Just a few Democrats spoke forcefully for the bill. No Republicans stood up to criticize a commission.

The invisible hand of Sen. Mitch McConnell, the Republican leader, was at work. He whipped his caucus into a state of stonewalling apathy.

So much for healing democracy. So much for banishing Trump from the realm, Mitch.

I got decidedly glum. The stakes were as high as they could be. What was missing from the drama: giants of the Senate.

Chatting with a leading Washington journalist, we recalled our rookie days when a number of senators were truly great speakers and statesmen.

It was a fun game.

As we waited for anything to happen, we named names from both sides, saying how lucky we were to cover the Senate then.

Daniel Webster was long gone, but the late Edward M. Kennedy was just as good. Both Massachusetts senators roared like lions and held the floor for hours.

Now the Senate had to deal with Trumpian Sen. Ron Johnson, a Wisconsin Republican, holding up business at 11 at night, suggesting a three-hour break so he could read new amendments.

Johnson made cheeks burn. To recover, I visited a Reception Room portrait of Robert LaFollette Sr., the Wisconsin Progressive and one of history's greats.

The morning vote was 54 for a commission, 35 opposed. But still, it failed under the filibuster rule of 60.

A long love was broken. The vote was not even the knell.

I never dreamt 11 senators would miss such an important vote to catch their planes. Kind of broke my heart.

The 4th Brings Us Back to Each Other

July 7, 2021

MADISON, Wis.—The fireworks from here to Washington sang of a country renewing its place in the world—and its sense of self. It was the most meaningful Fourth of July in memory, six months after the armed mob stormed the Capitol.

Democracy is making a remarkable recovery.

Seeing people in person again—like family—after 18 months was a shared experience for millions. Travel was hard, but the pandemic made pilgrims of us all.

Hardship darkened our doors and lives for so long that the Fourth was a light in the distance.

The genial Bidens hosted 1,000 people to celebrate. I heard several say what a salve it is to witness a warm family in the White House.

On her way out, Melania Trump destroyed the Rose Garden. With two weeks in his waning presidency, Donald Trump almost murdered American optimism and faith in government institutions and norms.

A peaceful transfer of power was under fire.

A wounded national spirit can't be tried in court, and we need it back. If you think back to the 20th century, optimism was once unquenchable.

So, we missed the Village Dance but enjoyed the Fourth of July in this Midwestern gem set on Lake Mendota. There was the 1929 vintage fire engine, the parade and the pool.

Competition was fierce in the egg toss. Good old-fashioned fun.

Like 40 million fellow travelers, I saw my family for the first time in 18 months on the holiday. We all changed in ways that can't be captured in texts and Zoom calls during the pandemic.

Children grew and adults, too, had COVID-19 written

on their faces or waistlines. The psychological returns aren't in yet. Let's say we have a fresh gratitude for human company after a social famine.

"Come join the fun and bring your neighbors, family, friends or total strangers." That's from the village news of a "normal celebration!"

That's it right there. The American spirit distilled into one sentence. We are by nature outgoing and outspoken people. It was hard to be kept apart, and devastating that loved ones were lost.

"It's so great to see other people," said Lila, a West High school student who works at the pool. As we spoke, the place was jammed with a mosaic of people sunning, swimming, playing, diving.

The teen came up to me to chat, with an open smile. I didn't know her, but it was a pleasure to talk to someone I didn't know by the bubbler.

My parents went to West. I once walked in the children's parade as the Statue of Liberty. My grandfather volunteered as a village ambulance driver. The village has a wildflower prairie garden. We moved west when I was 8, but I love Madison and its story still.

On my visit, I hear of the glacier that covered and shaped this land about 14,000 years ago.

The glacier's marks and stones give me a sense of history coming and going. The Black Hawk Indians lived here, too.

In 2021, not all is rosy, to be clear. This is not exactly another Era of Good Feelings. The hard feelings in the Capitol between Democrats and Republicans run rampant.

President Biden just ended a futile, lost war in Afghanistan after 20 years. What happens there now? Back to the Taliban.

Major infrastructure bills are now up in the Senate air. Lawmakers come back to work next week.

Voting rights are in peril, as a recent Supreme Court ruling shows. We are only starting to see what damage the three young justices named by Trump will do.

Oh, there is one more thing. Trump declared he'll be "reinstated" in August. That's next month. This may be idle chatter, but his threats about January 6 turned out to be true.

He incited and invited violence once and could do it twice.

We can't take anything for granted, for better or worse, now, not friends, family nor foes.

The Village Dance, "a great multi-generational event" will end, as always, with the FULL version of 'American Pie.'"

John Adams, who invented the Fourth's traditions, should come to Madison sometime.

The Search for Truth on Jan. 6 Brings Tears

July 28, 2021

WASHINGTON — I don't need a hearing to tell me what happened on Jan. 6 at the U.S. Capitol, which was stormed by an armed mob. But the nation needs a reckoning on that deadly day.

It was a moment history will never forget, a presidential attack on an equal branch of government, Congress. This I can tell you: It was not a drill, nor a sightseeing lark.

I felt something bad would happen, but there I was to witness the saddest story I've ever seen.

A House select committee held its first hearing Tuesday on the event. Four police officers gave heartrending testimony on their beatings, injuries and lasting trauma.

A Republican congressman, Adam Kinzinger of Illinois, was moved to tears.

"We never imagined this could happen," he said. "This was a democracy-defending moment."

Kinzinger and Rep. Liz Cheney of Wyoming were the only House Republicans serving on the panel, defying their party leaders.

The mob meant to lynch then-Vice President Mike Pence and make Speaker of the House Nancy Pelosi go the way of Henry VIII's second wife.

Pence and Pelosi were presiding over election rituals and barely made it to safety. Lawmakers scrambled to make it out alive.

So did we. I was in the House chamber, in the press gallery. We heard gunshots in the Speaker's Lobby as the mob tried to breach the chamber. I covered the streets of Baltimore for The Sun newspaper, but I have never heard shots before.

But I heard the steps and sounds of the mob on the marble floors of democracy's citadel. They breached the Senate floor and made it a mockery.

What was at stake: a peaceful transfer of power, the core of democracy. In a morning rally, then-President Donald Trump invited and incited the insurrection, knowing hordes of loyalists had come to Washington. In broad daylight, a dark conspiracy became clear.

The House and Senate had gathered to certify the results of the presidential election. It's in the Constitution.

Conditions were pretty perfect for a coup, as both houses were in a solemn joint session. Trump, the loser in the 2020 presidential election, intended to stay in office by force. He was beyond caring about casualties.

Meanwhile, the fury did not even sound human. The sound of breaking glass was even harder on our ears. Kristallnacht, the (Nazi) Night of Broken Glass, had crossed an ocean of time. This violent crowd, mostly white men, came from all corners of the country.

Some in the mob, with military experience, waged hand-to-hand combat with law enforcement. They hurled racial slurs at Black officers like stones of hate. Officer Harry Dunn told the panel he wept in the Rotunda that night.

That day, the U.S. Capitol Police were caught unprepared and lost control of the most precious building in the land, the people's house. The mob was coordinated — with gear, bear spray and weapons — as if they had cased the joint with help from their friends.

"This is because of you!" House Democrat Steve Cohen of Memphis, Tennessee, bellowed across the chamber to Republicans.

The Capitol Police tried to turn the tide but were overwhelmed by tens of thousands of rioters. Some actually scaled the walls. Some broke through locked doors. Hundreds commandeered the gorgeous terrace designed by Frederick Law Olmsted.

Ironically, Olmsted created it to make the Capitol more inviting to the people. If only the Central Park architect knew, he would weep. So would all our historical figures in marble and bronze inside.

There was no time to weep for us. The House chamber was locked, yet we knew we had to get out fast. Some journalists put on escape hoods. We had one exit to a secret staircase; House members had another. Soon we rushed down the same tunnel, hoping not to meet the mob on the other side.

The president's Pentagon was AWOL. If not for the District of Columbia Metropolitan Police sending 800 officers, the story would be sadder still.

So, we know what happened that damned day. Now the select committee must get to the bottom of who, why and how, Chairman Bennie Thompson, D-Mass., declared.

Not least of the things to investigate is Trump's role as instigator of the highest crime in presidential history.

Two Californias Clash in a Divided House: Pelosi Versus McCarthy

Aug. 4, 2021

WASHINGTON—It's a first in American history: The speaker of the House and the minority leader hail from the same state. But they barely speak.

Two Californias dwell and dominate in the House of Representatives. The party leaders, House Speaker Nancy Pelosi, D-Calif., and Kevin McCarthy, R-Calif., live in diametrically opposed worlds within the same state: the blue coastal liberals versus the rural inland "empire," largely red.

I know, coming from California, that Pelosi and McCarthy perfectly reflect her San Francisco and his Bakersfield. They are connected by a long ride on Interstate 5, cutting through the heart of the state.

This tension is not the known Northern versus Southern California culture rift, but the deep political fault lines between East and West in the Golden State.

The twain are getting farther apart. Seldom have House party leaders so openly scorned each other. McCarthy refers to Pelosi as a "lame-duck speaker." The House is so evenly divided—a few votes apart—the balance of power could change in a few heartbeats.

The drama between Pelosi and McCarthy plays out in the full House over burning issues: the Jan. 6 attack on the Capitol and COVID-19.

After first stating then-President Donald Trump "bears responsibility" for directing the armed mob, McCarthy deflected blame from him, even suggesting the speaker was responsible for the spectacular security breakdown.

This was an unkind cut, given the pack was hunting her.

So, let's set the scene between the two players. Days ago, Pelosi was overheard saying McCarthy is "a moron" in the thick of summer heat and partisan battle.

McCarthy then told donors Sunday it would be "hard not to hit" Pelosi with the speaker's gavel if he captures it. Very nice to threaten violence.

This fits his smug fraternity guy persona, one who can't stand a woman—81 to his 56—blocking his path to that precious gavel.

The man from Bakersfield is craven in pursuit of that speaker's (majority) gavel, willing to say about anything, however uncivil or uncouth.

McCarthy was bitter, perhaps, that Pelosi outwitted him on selecting members for a committee to investigate the storming of the House and Senate chambers—and whether it was orchestrated by Trump. He picked five Republicans. One was notorious Jim Jordan of Ohio, a vehement Trump supporter.

Pelosi nixed Jordan and another aggressive critic of the investigation, Jim Banks, R-Ind. Furious, McCarthy boycotted the committee, which he opposed in the first place.

That left two House Republicans willing to serve on the committee. Pelosi named Liz Cheney of Wyoming and Adam Kinzinger of Illinois. McCarthy may throw more shade and political revenge their way, but for now they have some high ground in the House, if not in their caucus.

Less becoming was a press conference McCarthy gave with a throng of anti-masker members of Congress. On the Capitol's east steps, the aggrieved Californian ripped Pelosi's decision (based on medical advice) to mandate masks on the House floor again in light of the raging delta variant.

Before the House adjourned for August recess, a brigade of McCarthy's maskless members, including the flinty Marjorie Taylor Greene, R-Ga., marched over to the Senate chamber in a ploy to call attention to their pandemic plight. I ran right into them, a breathless moment because I was in the building on Jan. 6.

Amusing that the Senate was too busy working on infrastructure to entertain the House callers.

Pelosi, once the Baltimore mayor's daughter, brings an artful skill to dealings with diverse Democrats and foreign leaders alike. She stays ahead of the Senate by a country mile, passing progressive bills such as the Voting Rights Act.

As a history major, I enjoy her keen grasp of Abraham Lincoln, Benjamin Franklin and woman suffrage leaders.

McCarthy may be speaker someday, but that's all he wants. His ideas for the greater good are not nearly as clear as his raw ambition.

It's not complicated: McCarthy feels he needs Trump for that end. So, as he shamelessly shifts ground, he's handing the scheming former president power over the 2022 election.

On a lighter note, Pelosi and McCarthy are both good-looking. They could play themselves in a movie. This is California, after all.

The Tragic March of 2021: Will It Ever End Well?

Aug. 18, 2021

WASHINGTON — The year 2021 is so far framed by the Jan. 6 U.S. Capitol riot and the Aug. 15 fall of Afghanistan without firing a shot.

In a momentous march of malady, misfortune and strife, we also witnessed a second presidential impeachment trial; the comeback of COVID-19; the collapse of a condominium high-rise in Florida; a New York governor rightfully forced out of office; the climate crisis declared to be here to stay and getting worse; a devastating earthquake in Haiti, with a hurricane closing in; and then desperate chaos in Kabul, Afghanistan's capital city, as the Taliban moved in and we moved out after 20 years.

Just for the record, July was the hottest month ever recorded on our planet Earth.

You add it all up, and it equals an epoch, a sad season beyond belief. Such a tragic year stays encoded in people's minds and memories over time. The dark year of the deadly plague and Great Fire in London, 1666, is still remembered.

Let's look at some of the days we've just lived through. The sight of Afghan civilians fleeing toward a cargo plane, and the hasty evacuation of American embassy staff, was a rude shock. Not a good look.

President Joe Biden's ringing defense of his decision to leave a quagmire begun by former President George W. Bush was fair enough. But I know it's heartbreaking for the military who served there to think of the translators and other friends left to the ruthless Taliban. Women and girls may return to an enslaved status, no different than 20 years ago.

One more lost war, after Vietnam. A veteran diplomat, the late Richard Holbrooke, warned former President Barack Obama that Afghanistan was beginning to look a lot like

Vietnam. This was a dozen years ago. Obama literally laughed at him and started a surge.

But more American soldiers were never going to turn the useless Afghan army and police into a fighting force, we know now. All the gleaming weapons the United States gave away now belong to the Taliban, firmly in control of the reclaimed country.

How humiliating, an epic failure by the generals, three presidents and all the foreign policy experts who spun a fiction about how things were going on the ground. Suddenly, there's no story left to tell except the truth.

Two trillion dollars later, Bush spends time on his Texas ranch painting portraits of injured soldiers among thousands of casualties on the rugged land of mountains and caves. A kind of penance.

Michael K. Gould spent a year deployed to Afghanistan as an Army judge advocate. He observed an impossible mission: "That (year) really opened my eyes to the folly of nation building in a poor, remote, tribalized country where the majority of the people are illiterate and hostile or, at best, indifferent to the goals of the occupation, and where the leaders are massively corrupt.

"This was never going to end well," he said simply.

The end was eerily like the American farewell to Vietnam.

But here at home, the truth is Afghanistan never occupied us. "In two weeks, nobody is going to remember this," my father said.

Besides, we're busy with mask and vaccine mandates as children go back to school and some adults return to the workplace. The brief burst of freedom in June, when the Centers for Disease Control and Prevention decreed the end of the mask era, made us giddy—then wary as the summer case numbers started climbing.

The rising number of new COVID-19 cases—about 130,000 daily—is enough to make you swear off states like

Florida for life. Standoffs between the masked and maskless are politicized in the worst way.

That brings me to Jan. 6. I was in the room, the House Chamber. I heard the mob break glass in the marble halls. Then a shattering gunshot in the Speaker's Lobby. Members of Congress and the press escaped into lockdown for untold hours.

I knew Congress was divided. But I didn't know how much raw anger and violence was out there. It was the first time the creamy marble citadel of American democracy was ever attacked.

That was only the beginning.

Diary Notes:
Washington Puts a Dark Past To Rest

Sept. 15, 2021

WASHINGTON — The city starts a new season, after Sept. 11 remembrances. Congress returns from summer recess. In the Capitol press gallery, you hear a bubbly chatter as if we're going back to school, a new beginning.

Could we be turning a corner from a mob storming the Capitol, an impeachment trial and the pandemic? As a witness to all three within these marble walls and halls, I so want to say yes.

Let me share some diary notes from the dome.

The lost war in Afghanistan colored the elegiac 9/11 moments — since that day led to the war. The high-noon sun beat down on House Speaker Nancy Pelosi and other leaders gathered on the Capitol's East Front steps.

The Speaker had the Marine Band play "God Bless America" for old time's sake. Twenty years ago, Congress sang that song as the sun set on 9/11.

Abraham Lincoln was inaugurated on those very steps. The dome he built was the target of the doomed United Flight 93 plane, which passengers forced to the ground.

Nearby, Secretary of State Antony Blinken gamely faced a committee pitching hardballs on the chaotic Afghanistan withdrawal.

"We inherited a deadline (from former President Donald Trump)," Blinken said. "We did not inherit a plan."

Years ago, Tony told me what a government "principal" was. Now he is one.

Across the plaza, a gleaming building bears the motto, "Equal Justice Under Law." Very nice.

The Supreme Court upheld a Texas law that a former law clerk for the late Justice Antonin Scalia invented, letting vigilantes loose on reproductive rights.

At midnight, the unsigned opinion was joined by the only woman on the anti-woman side, once a "handmaid" in her religion, Justice Amy Coney Barrett. She who stole onto the Court while Ruth Bader Ginsburg's body cooled in the parlor, days before the 2020 election.

As burned as we are at the Supreme Court, Texas earns even more ire. The statehouse retrenched voting rights this summer, at the governor's urging. Gov. Greg Abbott is also a sworn enemy of COVID-19 vaccine mandates.

The Lone Star State is its own country. So, Texas, you're invited to secede. I wouldn't miss you. Lincoln opposed letting the largest slave state into the Union in the first place.

Rays of light smiled on a standout weekend night by the Lincoln Memorial and the Reflecting Pool. Thousands gathered to picnic at a free concert of the Broadway musical, "Come from Away."

It tells the true story of 7,000 airline travelers landing in Gander, Newfoundland, on 9/11. They were bedraggled on a "giant piece of rock in the middle of the ocean." The townspeople welcomed strangers from all over the world into their homes and hearts.

Thanks, Ford's Theatre, for this dreamy gift, a tonic to raise a glass to Canada. The scene was the happiest I'd seen the city in so long.

Next morning, I went to a funeral mass for an ink-stained editor, Al Eisele. He was a friend to all by name: the barista, news agent, homeless guy, deli owner.

On 9/11, Al's friend David McCullough, the historian, was over at the fancy Hay-Adams Hotel. He called Al and said, why don't you come over here?

Al brought two young reporters to witness the towers fall and the Pentagon burn with McCullough—and wrote a column about it.

Back in the press gallery, a police officer passed by, back from a wartime deployment. "I was safer in Afghanistan (than here) on Jan. 6," he said.

That sank an arrow in our banter. That happened: 140 police officers injured in the Capitol melee. We heard gunshots right by the House chamber.

The saddest siege ended before dawn. Democracy won, but not by much.

They say the Trump mob is coming back Saturday. Deport them to Texas or Gander.

As the fall season starts, Democrats need every player on the field, like that former quarterback, Sen. Joe Manchin of West Virginia. They are thinking big, real New Deal lawmaking aimed at the future.

Lincoln led us out of the dark toward the light.

It's in the air, a clear chance to go further forward.

Biden Needs to Keep Away Skunks and Mobs

Oct. 13, 2021

WASHINGTON — The Biden presidency hangs not upon the House, but two Democratic senators, skunks at the political garden party. As skies darken, the Jan. 6 Capitol mob comes closer. These ominous signs are related.

I heard shrieks and howls while in the House chamber. It was an armed, bloodthirsty bunch. Footsteps and broken glass on pristine marble marked their trail.

I love history, but not witnessing that black day's descent. And former President Donald Trump's sedition is not done.

His mob is not history. The worst loser of all time will not leave us in peace. We're wrong to let Trump roam the land freely (when under investigation) and incite Iowans.

One national security expert, Fiona Hill, called Jan. 6 a "dress rehearsal." Mark Milley, Chairman of the Joint Chiefs, made the same point, knowing the mind of the president he served.

Chilling when you think the Capitol's only other attack was when British soldiers sacked it in 1814, a legitimate act of war.

The wheels of Justice turn slowly. Attorney General Merrick Garland's department has made less than 700 arrests. The crowd that day outnumbered Trump's 2017 inauguration. Light sentences suggested by prosecutors troubled some judges.

Trump appealed to his Justice Department nine times to undo his lost election.

Nobody could make up the ninth time. Meeting with top government lawyers, including one who defended him at an impeachment trial, Trump hit a wall when they threatened to resign.

Note the date was Jan. 3, 2021. Trump had one last card to play. Three days later came a cunning, coordinated plot to storm the Capitol while Congress was ratifying the Electoral College win for President Joe Biden. Jan. 6 is named in the Constitution.

The House and Senate were captive in the Capitol.

What a perfect setup for tens of thousands who descended on our town from all points, as far away as California and Texas. They were not tourists. They did not come at a moment's notice. One brought bear spray.

The House Select Committee on Jan. 6 is at work issuing subpoenas—one to Trump's chief of staff, Mark Meadows—and piecing the truth together. The FBI was late to the game again.

This much is clear: The conspiracy took weeks, even months, to organize. The mob knew which Capitol doors to break down. They scaled the walls. They must have cased the joint, because they knew where to go.

The mob missed the Senate by moments. Vice President Mike Pence, presiding over the count, escaped a mass lynching. As bad as it was, it could have been a murderous bloodbath. Some in the House chamber fled down a secret staircase.

Bearded faces poked through beautiful broken glass doors during a gun standoff. I covered Baltimore for years and never heard shots fired in anger.

The Capitol Police were helped by 800 members of the Metropolitan Police, in hand-to-hand combat. It's not pretty, what the white mob called officers of color.

Trump is not done with those of us who hold democracy dear, fond of a peaceful transfer of power.

He learned from his sordid life that if he keeps saying something over and over in his ferocious way, that he can fool some of the people all of the time.

From Queens real estate to depraved Roman Empire days in the White House, that's what he lives on, a banquet of lies and Big Macs.

Trump makes angry people believe his junk.

To this day, his party feeds at the banquet of lies, even old Iowa Sen. Charles Grassley. The media indulges his House lackeys, asking if they believe Biden won the election. How insane.

Democracy won, but not by much. We wept at the end of the siege.

2021 isn't done with us yet. Sens. Joe Manchin of West Virginia and Kyrsten Sinema of Arizona are the lone Democrats hurting Biden every day they delay on his legislative agenda.

Sen. Bernie Sanders, I-Vt., says it's "not fair" for a few in a 50-member caucus to thwart a major bill—Build Back Better, with improvements for climate change, Medicare and child care.

To hold Trump at bay, Biden needs sunlight, not skunks, at his garden party.

At Thanksgiving, Democracy on the Table

Nov. 24, 2021

Thanksgiving is all about saving the Union from forces that almost destroyed it. President Abraham Lincoln proclaimed it a national holiday in 1863, midway through the benighted Civil War.

November defines turning points in the most tragic hours of history.

Lincoln gave the Gettysburg Address on the battlefield of that great war on Nov. 19, 1863, once the cannonballs were silenced and the dead buried. Gen. Robert E. Lee's cocky rebel army was depleted. For the Civil War president, victory at Gettysburg was the beginning of the end.

Now as we pilgrims feast in 2021, that meaning remains clear as day. There is a sense of huge losses and precious gains at our shared tables. It's fair to say we civilians felt besieged as if at war.

This Thursday in November, we're still in the grip of a global pandemic. We're also haunted by the sixth day of this year. The body politic is scarred from a civil war waged within, a violent blow to American democracy by a mob incited by a president.

I was there, but in a larger sense all who love democracy were inside its citadel. The coup failed, but believe me, it was a close call.

By proclamation from war-torn Washington, the first national Thanksgiving (a New England tradition) was marked in November 1863. Lincoln was grateful to providence—and perhaps Gen. George Meade—for winning the Battle of Gettysburg in July. By the Fourth, the smoke cleared.

That narrow win over Lee was the catalyst for celebrating the autumn holiday and the greatest piece of presidential prose. In five elegiac minutes, Lincoln stood and redefined the raging war.

Suddenly, the meaning was "a new birth of freedom" from slavery. For Lincoln himself was profoundly changed.

His battlefield utterance went beyond the Union map to the meaning of the "unfinished work" of freedom. Standing on the ground of enormous human suffering, in the crucible of war, he honored the dead and inspired the living.

The world often notes that Lincoln was not an abolitionist when he ran for president in 1860. True, yet the lanky prairie lawyer became the greatest abolitionist of all. To transform a nation, the revolution came from within.

This year, as President Joe Biden labored to lead the nation out of despair in a double calamity, we have not heard a soaring address. But the pain we were in was often written on his face and felt in his voice.

Biden is, above all, sincere. Never have we needed that more after the other president traded only in lies, boasts and insults.

I might add, Biden is much more thoughtful and wise than the loquacious senator who served for 35 years. He's undergone a transformation as a public man, perhaps by mourning his son Beau. Lincoln also lost a beloved son while in office.

Sworn in with a bitterly divided House and Senate, shattered social bonds and a chorus of critics (a White House Washington Post reporter tweeted his agenda was "dying"), Biden achieved improbable victories this very month.

First, he signed a regular infrastructure bill with bipartisan support.

A social infrastructure bill—from universal pre-K to home health care—finally united House Democrats for a narrow victory that seems solid enough to sail into the 50-50 Senate with high hopes.

Call it Biden's Gettysburg. If the second—Build Back Better—becomes law, it will transform middle- and working-class lives and address the climate crisis.

On a bright morning after eight hours of House

Republican Leader Kevin McCarthy of California shouting into the night, House Speaker Nancy Pelosi, D-Calif., was the finest field general Biden could have, gaveling the 220-213 vote.

Finally, the day President John F. Kennedy died was Nov. 22, 1963, one century after the 1863 Gettysburg Address. Is it just chance that Jack Kennedy, son of Massachusetts, was slain in Texas, the largest Confederate slave state?

Lincoln opposed admitting Texas to the Union. Kennedy had to win the Jim Crow state to win reelection. The murdered presidents reach across time with intertwined fates.

November brings darkest days but may leave a light of hope at the table.

Democracy wins, but not by much, over those trying to tear us apart.

The Trump Contagion Still Spreading

Dec. 8, 2021

WASHINGTON — The worst contagion still spreading is not the omicron nor the delta variant of the deadly coronavirus. This medical contagion has claimed more than 750,000 American lives since March 2020 and laid the rest of us low.

The contagion I mean is clear and ever more dangerous: Donald Trump.

The social scourge the ex-president started spreading from his first day in office is arguably worse than the pandemic.

Now we know Trump came into contact with 500 people when he knew he had COVID-19. He flew with COVID-19. He recklessly refused to wear a mask. He debated then-candidate Joe Biden.

Trump gave people the plague, no doubt, in White House and campaign events. If only it were that simple. Then we could shut the book of history on the 45th president.

In that book, we'd record Trump showed contempt for the looming pandemic by visiting the Centers for Disease Control and Prevention in golf attire and a red "Make America Great Again" cap last winter. As author Bob Woodward reported, he ignored expert advice, though he told Woodward how catching the airborne virus was.

Why a president led the American people into the waters of death, loss and grief is a question for the ages. Surely the plague would have been contained — or lessened — by any responsible, decent man in the Oval Office.

How I dream on for that outcome. For a nation where fights don't break out on planes over masks. A vaccinated sweet land of reason.

Trump dirtied the American body politic with hate, grievance and lies, which culminated in the horrifying mob he incited to storm the Capitol on Jan. 6.

It was not just a violent Trump farewell party. As I witnessed gunfire inside the Capitol, I felt a fury unleashed, a beast that could not be stopped in a single day by law enforcement.

That was the attempted murder of our democracy.

It was then beyond our imagination, though I knew foul play would happen that wintry day. I felt it in the air.

Tens of thousands, mostly middle-aged white men, amassed into the armed mob. Not even 700 have yet been charged. The longest sentence so far, meted out to the savage horned and helmeted rioter, Jacob Chansley, is less than four years. I went to the courthouse to see him face the judge.

The Charlottesville, Virginia, race riot in August 2017 was a prelude.

That ugly street scene, and Trump's defending "very fine" white supremacists, foretold our worst traits coming out into the open.

With Trump's low vernacular speech, a scorn for women, bloodcurdling racism and toxic xenophobia burst into our common spaces. Soon after, the public square burned to the ground, with "social media" lighting matches.

The most unforgivable thing Trump did is bring out the worst in us. Call it public "discoarse." This is most evident among the House of Representatives' Republicans. A sorry lot, they love Trump or quake in fear of him.

This gun-lovin' group has no shame. The rules are that there are no rules. They openly threaten violence, recently in a cartoon anime tweet by the outrageous Rep. Paul Gosar, R-Ariz., against a young Democratic congresswoman of color. Gosar had to stand in the floor well to be censured by Speaker Nancy Pelosi, D-Calif., and the full House.

Reps. Lauren Boebert, R-Colo., and Marjorie Taylor Greene, R-Ga., are Trumpian freshmen whose unlettered gutter talk would shock any other House.

On Jan. 6, Boebert hinted at the gathering riot in a floor speech: "Madam Speaker, I have constituents outside the building right now."

The Trump scourge is spreading to statehouses to skew the midterm elections. Revenge is upon us all.

Even if Trump never seizes power, his poisoning the public well will last generations. He appointed three young radical Republicans to the Supreme Court, all enemy to reproductive rights, the law of the land.

The old Republican senator and soldier, Bob Dole, tragically died this week as a "Trumper." Indeed, that was the death knell of the grand old party.

Aftermath

Jamie Stiehm

Seven Senators Who Go Back to Civil War Days

Dec. 15, 2021

WASHINGTON — When I walk by John Calhoun in the Capitol, I stare at his severe portrait and ask, are you happy now with democracy cracking up? And I swear the ghost says yes, fire burning in his eyes.

Make no mistake, this Southern senator isn't a vestige of the antebellum past. Calhoun's spirit still roams the halls in several Republican senators. Starting with the Capitol riot and siege on Jan. 6, this truth became painfully clear.

Let me name seven names here. House Republicans are full of malice and mischief, but senators should not escape scrutiny while the House select committee investigates the Jan. 6 conspiracy.

Calhoun of South Carolina (of course) was the architect and instigator of the Civil War, though he never lived to see the day. On his deathbed in 1850, the pro-slavery zealot precisely predicted how it would come. He was a prophet of doom, blood and violence against the republic.

With current cleavages in Congress breaking roughly along Civil War lines, Calhoun would be downright delighted at our divided nation. What's the difference between an armed insurrection and a rebel army, after all? Each waged war on the state from within.

Today, Sen. Ted Cruz of Texas wins first place for aggressive acts against the government, lately blocking some of President Joe Biden's ambassadorial nominees.

Worse, in the last act of the Jan. 6 tragedy, Cruz had the nerve to challenge the certification of Biden's victory in the dark morning hours. As if courting an audience of one: glowering loser Donald Trump.

Nobody likes Cruz, who represents the largest Confederate slave state. Calhoun was just like him: single-minded in opposition at every turn. Calhoun developed doctrines of secession and "nullification," meaning states could — and should — defy and break from the federal government if their sacred slavery was threatened.

President Andrew Jackson made the best comment of his cruel life when he said his only regret was not hanging his vice president, Calhoun.

Cruz was a champion debater at Princeton. Calhoun relentlessly argued for the "peculiar institution," to put it politely, justifying slavery from his Yale days on. Kindred spirits.

Arrogant freshman Sen. Josh Hawley, another Yalie, raised his fist to the gathering pro-Trump mob outside the Capitol. I walked past them, too, on the stately grounds and felt my bones chill.

Hawley was raised on Rush Limbaugh hate talk in their shared home state, Missouri, a slave state.

Hawley's looks are clean-cut, but his heart is dark. Like Cruz, he brazenly challenged the presidential election count hours after the mob sacked the temple of democracy.

What did their fancy Ivy educations teach these men? At least, Yale recently scrubbed Calhoun's name from a residential college.

I might add, Rick Scott of Florida was a Southern Senate Republican who challenged the constitutional count and prolonged the agony of the worst day Americans witnessed in the Capitol. (It was deserted when the British army burned it in 1814 in an act of war.)

I'm making a list of others, checking it twice.

Also among the truly awful Republican senators are: Lindsey Graham of South Carolina, Rand Paul of Kentucky, Ron Johnson of Wisconsin and John Barrasso of Wyoming.

Since his House days, Graham is totally unprincipled and recently, strikingly slavish toward Trump. He needs a strongman in his life.

All are masters of insolence. Paul insulted Dr. Anthony

Fauci at a COVID-19 committee hearing. Johnson is trying to undermine his own state election rules, following the script set forth on Jan. 6. Strident Barrasso cuts up Biden constantly, like the surgeon he is.

Up-and-coming Republicans are freshmen Sens. Roger Marshall of Kansas and Bill Hagerty of Tennessee: big troublemakers in waiting.

Yes, I'm giving Republican Leader Mitch McConnell of Kentucky a pass. Burning the Capitol to the ground is not his way. And anybody Trump hates as an old "crow" can't be all bad.

Calhoun declared any president opposed to slavery's expansion would see a civil war break out. That president was prairie newcomer Abraham Lincoln, elected a decade later. War was started by Calhoun's home state.

170 years after he lay dying, Calhoun's true political heir is a confederate named Trump.

The Kindness of New Yorkers as Christmas Came Near

Dec. 22, 2021

WASHINGTON — New York was full of kind strangers two weeks before Christmas, even as the omicron variant was coming to town.

A police officer in the 14th Street subway saw me carrying two travel bags and without a word, swiped me in free with a smile.

Just moments earlier, I chatted with two outgoing young men at a juice bar. They extolled the strong ginger shots and gulped them down as a daily ritual.

"My treat," one said. "Try it."

"Next time," I said, feeling a buzzy jolt of Christmas cheer, sorry I had to board the train back to the political wars in Washington.

As a journalist in the Capitol press gallery when the mob held Congress under siege on Jan. 6, I carried some scars on my shoulders the rest of the year.

The coup de grace came in the elevator in my college friend's apartment building on Riverside Park. We were set to walk across Central Park that Sunday afternoon and go to the Metropolitan Museum of Art.

I was wearing my best coat, a London leopard print, trying not to look like a country cousin. An elegant woman, Maxine, in the elevator said she had a coat she thought would look good on me.

When we returned hours later, a beautiful coat was hanging on M's doorknob. It fit me perfectly. It was my Christmas coat.

What was in the air? A California friend said, "you radiate good karma." Another said, "restorative kindness."

The unbidden encounters might be just luck. But I don't think so. What struck me was that none made much ado of being generous. They just acted easily, as if it was totally natural to befriend a stranger.

And it did me a world of good. No kidding, New York felt like a drink of cold well water after the Capitol's parched clime. The high spirits of social democracy were at play. This was more like it, America.

The Capitol, which I frequent on both House and Senate sides, now feels like an armed camp. Things were bad before Jan. 6, don't get me wrong. But the near-misses of the violent marauders—tens of thousands of them—colored the place with party fury, fear and frustration at record levels.

The second impeachment trial of former President Donald Trump (for the Jan. 6 riot) sapped any bipartisan goodwill left to greet a new president.

West Virginia Sen. Joe Manchin's dramatic betrayal of President Joe Biden's Build Back Better social policy deal was the bitter end to the most bitter draft of American politics since the Civil War broke out. The rioters were Confederates.

Without fully knowing it, I carried a case of battle fatigue to New York.

It's no secret that New Yorkers suffered greatly during the pandemic's first wave in 2020. Many were confined indoors in smaller spaces. Street life was all but dead.

The city came through it, sailing and shining. The lines into the Met flooded the steps. An Afro-futurist period room, co-curated by another college friend, was the rage. The neighborhood diner was booming, with proof of vaccination required. Cheese blintzes were the order of the day. Earlier, the Broadway church service bonded all kinds and made me teary for the year's losses.

Did I see the last December dance before another long, hard winter? Nobody knows what's next. We're in an age of unpleasant surprises.

What I do know: I was warmed by the kindness of others in New York. The city's heart of gold may hide under a gruff manner. But it's there, perhaps softened by the social desert wrought by the coronavirus.

One more count against Trump: His rude, brash hucksterism was often chalked up to being an iconic New York type. Nah. He's a pariah in New York and hangs out in Florida, where the water's warmer for his type.

New York's humanity was on display in the days before Christmas. I've got the coat to prove it, catching the joy of living.

The 21st Century: A Flop So Far

Dec. 29, 2021

A child in the '60s, when the world was turning fast, I loved the upbeat '90s' carbonated peace and prosperity. But the 2020s are a bitter brew of COVID-19 and poison politics choking us.

In fact, the 21st century lost the plot early on.

George W. Bush was a tragic tiebreaker choice of president by the Supreme Court. Bush v. Gore, a 5-4 ruling in 2000, gave new meaning to "one man, one vote." The supremely political Court ruled against the people's popular vote.

One event led to another in a cascade that has made all the difference. Once, even globalization sounded good.

If you believe in harbingers, things haven't been the same since. If you recall Bush's rookie reaction to the terrorist attacks of Sept. 11, it was wide-eyed fear: "Oh dang, that's the plane plot the CIA briefer told me about in August when I was clearing brush in Crawford." (A paraphrase.)

Bush was utterly unprepared for a simple plan he should have seen coming. Somehow, he got away with it. Outgoing President Bill Clinton told him that al-Qaida was his biggest national security problem, words he ignored. So did Condoleezza Rice, his national security adviser.

We were shattered after Sept. 11. Bush preyed on this dark moment and changed our way of life with domestic surveillance, torture of suspected terrorists and a behemoth agency called "homeland security." This made airports and other public spaces ugly and forbidding.

The White House now looks like a fortress and Congress built a bunker.

Seeking revenge, Bush started two wars of aggression, in Afghanistan and Iraq. Thousands of lives were lost and trillions were spent on lost wars. The United States left these nations in shambles, Afghanistan back to the benighted

Taliban.

The war in Iraq was waged on Bush's false claims of "weapons of mass destruction." There were no ties between Iraqi dictator Saddam Hussein and the Sept. 11 hijackers, mostly Saudi nationals. By then, we had crossed the Tigris and the Euphrates.

To make matters worse, Bush won a close contest in 2004 against Sen. John Kerry, a Vietnam War hero who led veterans opposing the war. Bush had no such proud record and allowed Kerry to be painted poorly by "Swift Boat" veterans. That was when truth became a casualty in presidential politics.

Al Gore and Kerry were leading environmentalists who would have plowed ahead on climate change. Just sayin'.

In 2008, a dazzling young Black president was elected amid a financial crisis that rocked the housing industry: the Great Recession. The new president did not punish Wall Street wrongdoers who caused the debacle. We saw the wordsmith avoid confrontation, a missing element in his chemistry.

For a while, Barack Obama's oratory pleased the people.

But the 44th president prolonged Bush's wars. He passed Obamacare, but fell short on the environment, immigration and gun control. Racial police violence went unchecked.

Finally, Obama let a Supreme Court seat get away, never calling out Senate Majority Leader Mitch McConnell, R-Ky., for blocking his nominee. A president can't let a senator humiliate him. That is just what Obama did.

Obama prided himself on being bipartisan and named Republican James Comey his FBI director. Comey foiled Hillary Clinton's presidential quest not once, but twice, for investigations that came to nothing.

Clinton's loss was also Obama's. He failed to protect his legacy. The solo artist in politics—a rare bird—did not campaign enough to get his chosen one elected in 2016.

The crowning blow to the century so far was Donald Trump—the angry anti-Obama who took power after losing the popular vote. He was impeached twice, very nice.

Trump's vile tweets, vulgar boasts and virulent lies he told as part of his job description sullied — and sickened — the American square almost beyond repair.

And then the rabble came for us — peaceful democracy — on Jan. 6, 2021.

I shall be telling this with a sigh, counting losses but believing in the dream that is America, still.

Senate Sets Stage for Showdown on Voting Rights

Jan. 12, 2022

The Capitol candlelight vigil for the mob attack on Congress gave way to a Senate showdown on voting rights—a scene straight from the heart of darkness.

Timed for the Martin Luther King Jr. holiday, it's a showdown Senate Democrats don't know they can win. But they have to try, for a fair field in the upcoming midterms. Plus, it's a great chance for Sen. Joe Manchin, D-W.Va., who plays Hamlet to the hilt, to choose "to be" with his own party.

President Joe Biden gave a speech in Georgia Tuesday, urging the Senate to change its filibuster rules, if necessary, to restore voting rights. That prospect has Senate Republicans breathing fire.

But the heart of darkness is across the street from the Capitol: the Supreme Court. While the Capitol endured a physical brutal assault, the Court often tears down the walls of democracy from inside.

In 2013, the Court struck down a shiny pearl from the civil rights era: the Voting Rights Act. That's the reason why the Senate is in the crosshairs now. The activist Supreme Court acts in all the wrong ways—with more to come.

Chief Justice John Roberts and other Republicans waged war on a widely praised voting rights law, applied to the South where patterns of racial discrimination persist. The infamous case was brought by Shelby County, Alabama, and brought the late Justice Ruth Bader Ginsburg's strongest dissent.

Senate Democratic Leader Chuck Schumer declared, "Everyone in this chamber will have a chance to go on record ... on defending democracy." Since the Jan. 6 siege, he says, voter suppression laws are on the rise.

Senate Republican Leader Mitch McConnell, canny and shrewd, says a rule change on the 60-vote filibuster would "break the Senate." Why, heavens above, Democrats want to "federalize elections."

Yes, Mitch. Federal offices should be subject to federal oversight laws, as they were for nearly 50 years. Presidential and congressional elections by right need federal backbone and should not be left to uneven states.

In the darkness of the "big lie" loser former President Donald Trump has spread (that the 2020 election was stolen), the urgency of passing a new Voting Rights Act is here and now. The Supreme Court left democracy with no umbrella in the rain, no winter coat on an arctic day.

Roberts is not even the worst Republican on the high court. Among the three Trump appointees, Brett Kavanaugh himself egged on a "preppie riot" as Florida votes were counted in the deadlocked Bush v. Gore election.

America got by for a cycle or two. The 2020 election was free and fair, by all accounts, with high turnout that looked like nonviolent resistance to me, multitudes standing in long lines. Biden won decisively.

But 19 states have just changed their voting laws and made it harder to register and to vote. Several Republican Trump loyalists are running for secretary of state, the office responsible for vote-counting. This means state electors may be more partisan instead of neutral. In Georgia, it will now be illegal to give water to voters waiting in line.

This is happening in plain view since the attempted murder of a peaceful democracy on Jan. 6, 2021.

The senator with the most at stake is the Rev. Raphael Warnock, D-Ga., pastor at the Ebenezer Baptist Church, where King preached. He's on the ballot again, after an upset win in 2020. In fiery floor speeches, he states nothing matters more in American democracy than protecting the rights of minority voters.

The Supreme Court gave us campaigns with unlimited "dark money," in Citizens United. It restricted a constitutional right to reproductive freedom in Texas. Employer mask mandates are at risk.

    Just you wait for the crux: whether the Court will allow the release of Trump's records from during the Jan. 6 siege.

    See what I mean? I rest my case.

Biden Meets the Moment in the House

March 2, 2022

WASHINGTON — FROM THE HOUSE LIVE

"The high honor ... of presenting to you, the President of the United States!" — House Speaker Nancy Pelosi

Showtime. The State of the Union rituals quell doubts the nation can long endure. There's no love lost across the aisle in the House of Representatives chamber, nor in the evenly divided Senate over on the Capitol's other side.

But for this one night, lawmakers are all here, banishing memories of the Jan. 6, 2021, mob. So is the Cabinet and the Pentagon brass. The Supreme Court was expected to attend, though only five showed. A fresh foreign policy crisis in Ukraine is underway just as the pandemic wanes.

President Joe Biden is right where he needs to be in a crisis presidency: center stage, speaking straight over his foes in the hall to the American people and the free world.

"We are going to be OK" is no fancy flight of Obama-esque oratory. But you know, that's OK. Biden is more believable, if you want to know the truth.

Just Joe and you, Joe and me, in his warm, direct voice, calling for praise and aid for the besieged people of Ukraine. "Pure courage," he said.

No longer just a "former comedian," President Volodymyr Zelensky won the world's heart by bravely facing the Russian onslaught of Ukraine.

"(Russian President Vladimir) Putin is more isolated than he has ever been," Biden declared, pleasing both sides of the House. American airspace will be closed to Russian planes, he announced, adding that NATO (the North Atlantic Treaty Organization) will keep its promise to defend every member nation.

Yet we live on tenterhooks on the first of March, as we ponder what the Russian war on Ukraine means for us. The unspoken question hanging over our heads: is Putin a mad man or a madman?

You tell me.

Zealous Putin, a former KGB spy, is driven by dreams of Mother Russia. American spy agencies need to read his mind better here and now, given reports that he seems changed and "strategically self-defeating," as an expert put it.

Back in the House, Sen. Joe Manchin, D-W. Va., was the sole Democrat sitting on the Republican side, hanging out with Mitt Romney, R-Utah. Bad optics, Joe.

Manchin is a dealbreaker in Biden's agenda for voting rights and his social infrastructure package, Build Back Better. In a 50-50 Senate, Democrats can't afford to lose one vote, a power the conservative Manchin uses liberally.

Biden pivoted to address the divide, the elephants and donkeys in the room.

"Let's stop seeing each other as enemies and start seeing each other for who we really are: Fellow Americans," Biden said. "We can't change how divided we've been. But we can change how we move forward."

Simple words, spoken to a chamber that seemed sobered up by how hard Ukrainians fought to hold onto their country, cities and land. They were showing us how much democracy meant.

Suddenly, the spirit lifted, less partisan than usual. I know, this wasn't my first rodeo.

On politics, the president smartly condemned the "Defund the Police" slogan and spoke up for corporate tax fairness. He wants downtowns to fill up again and hinted that social media companies, Big Tech, might be in for some regulation. Wouldn't that be nice.

Neighbors visiting from across the street (the Supreme Court) were harsh reminders that climate change and reproductive rights may rest in the high Court's hands.

The 6-3 radical Republican court has so much sway over us and is fully ready to use it.

Biden spoke of the two-year plague with the right sober touch: "We have lost so much to COVID-19. Time with one another. And worst of all, so much loss of life."

With that, Biden then reached up for the sky. "Now is the hour ... we will save democracy."

Gathered in the main chamber of democracy's heart, we could hear it beating better.

Biden is only the third president in American history to enter office as a "crisis president." Others were Abraham Lincoln confronting the Civil War and Franklin D. Roosevelt burdened with the Great Depression.

Lincoln and Roosevelt had surpassing skills as speakers. But this is no ordinary time, and the president is no ordinary Joe.

Trump Pecked and Plucked, Feather by Feather

March 16, 2022

The goose is getting fat.

We wait for his date on the dinner table after the plague, when the war is over. If it's over. This goose caused ravages in his riotous reign.

The goose's days as boss in barnyard politics are numbered. In back of his feathery head, he knows it. His pal, a vulture named Vladimir, is raining war, breaking a fragile peace.

It's no secret the goose and Vladimir were in cahoots. Now the world hates Vladimir. Honks about his savvy "genius" are gone from the goose.

Now you don't talk so loud/now you don't seem so proud.

Down south in Florida, where the goose is wintering, his troubles flew with him. They peck at his power.

It's tragically beautiful to watch the bird being plucked. Tragic because it's late in the day. The damage is done.

The metaphor fits Donald Trump, the former failed president who almost took democracy down. Not that he feels a pound of guilt in his folds of flesh. He just knows what he senses at any given moment in his coldblooded brain.

Right now, he feels his neck is in very real danger.

As president, Trump recklessly defied public health experts during the pandemic and inspired followers to do the same. Trump tore the social fabric apart (over masks) after COVID-19 descended in March 2020.

Most remember our last day before the public square went empty and silent. We mourn losses, little and large, in the saddest season.

While the nation's pestilence waned, Russia's invasion of Ukraine began. Yet justice for the Jan. 6 mob storming the Capitol is moving in the courts.

No other president pulled off all that trouble. Give the goose that.

Trump's lasting legacies shook the foundations not only of American health and democracy, but of NATO, too. We are within miles—and days?—of entering armed conflict with Russia on NATO ground in member country Poland. The treaty organization is sworn to defend the club.

Isn't that great? Like the Soviet Missile Crisis. That crisis was coolly handled by President John F. Kennedy while the world held its nuclear breath.

Trump's courting Russian President Vladimir Putin led to the present moment. They hatched a plan to weaken NATO first and for the United States to pull out in Trump's second term.

For his part, Putin hated the encirclement of small, new NATO countries near Russian borders. Albania, really? He viscerally rejected the idea that the large Ukraine, once part of the Soviet Union, would ever join NATO.

President Joe Biden and Western leaders refused to budge on that, leaving the door open to Ukraine joining NATO one day. That's what the war is all about. Sure hope it's worth it.

Emboldened or enraged, Putin invaded Ukraine. Possibly, he changed during the pandemic. Reports say he is isolated and irrational about restoring pieces of the old Soviet puzzle. The course of Russian history never did run smooth.

Ukrainian soldiers and citizens are facing or fleeing Russian bombs and tanks. President Volodymyr Zelenskyy, whom Trump tried to bribe in exchange for military aid, addressed a joint session of Congress Wednesday from his besieged land. He is a young David-like biblical figure.

Back at Mar-a-Lago, Trump is honking about Mike Pence, his vice-presidential Brutus, who condemned "apologists for Putin." That cut had to hurt.

Pence's finest hour was refusing to preside over Trump's scheme to undo the election on Jan. 6, 2021. When it counted, he saved American democracy from a violent overthrow.

There's much more to anger and alarm Trump. The Jan. 6 House committee is investigating whether he incited a criminal conspiracy.

Trump's accountants also disowned years of work for the Trump Organization. The New York attorney general is investigating its possible fraud. Candidates he's endorsed for Congress aren't sailing into the wind.

Steve Bannon, his inaugural advisor for the "American carnage" vision, goes on trial in July.

Having lost his potent political weapon, Twitter, Trump launched Truth Social. Only his most loyal disciples are talking it up.

Rep. Marjorie Taylor Greene, R-Ga., the most brazen of the bunch, is unpopular even among fellow Republicans.

The Trump presidency is like a goose close to being cooked.

Jamie Stiehm

Pelosi Makes Most of History Every Day

March 23, 2022

WASHINGTON—What do you know for women's history month? March is going fast. Quick, when did women win the vote?

"A Week in the Life of Speaker Pelosi" is my picture for the gallery.

The House speaker, a San Francisco Democrat, is a vivid historical figure who marches (excuse pun) onward every day, with the 222 House Democrats staying in sync.

Pelosi, the highest woman in American government, marks her 82nd birthday on March 26. She's told colleagues she'll step down at year's end—but will she? Should she?

That is the question. Pelosi led her party through the howling wilderness of Donald Trump's presidency. Now she's reaping fruits of a Democratic hold on the House, Senate and White House.

"Madam Speaker" is the only politician in Washington to confront ex-President Trump to his face. In fact, she was the decision-maker for his two impeachments and the Select Committee on the Jan. 6 storming of the beloved Capitol.

"Nothing surprises me," Pelosi likes to say. But the Trump mob that came for her—and her members—attacked democracy's citadel, like the Roman siege of the Temple in Jerusalem.

Beyond being a "first"—the first female speaker of the People's House—there's a steady fire and determination in her speech and stride that her friends love and her foes fear.

There she was at the NATO security conference in Germany last month as the Ukraine crisis unfolded.

Right in the middle of March, a look at Pelosi's calendar reveals a woman in the eye of our storms, bracketed by elegant events that made the Capitol glow and sing after a two-year pandemic winter.

"Nancy Pelosi is a remarkable leader who has managed to keep the House operating and her party together under the most extraordinarily difficult circumstances," Norm Ornstein, a leading expert on Congress, said.

The best, toughest speaker in history, Ornstein said. Period.

A March day in Statuary Hall: welcoming tennis great Billie Jean King, the trailblazer for women's equality in sports, was no small thing. Fifty years of Title IX was the toast of the hour. Pelosi invited the national champion girls basketball team, Sidwell Friends School.

The meringues, cupcakes and citrus drinks were beautiful to behold.

King spoke: "You never understand inclusion until you've been excluded."

I steered the willowy Sidwell "Quakers" to the suffrage statue and asked when women won the vote. They did not know — but that's not their fault. Ironically, the suffrage leaders were mostly Quakers.

The next day, Pelosi faced reporters asking why COVID-19 relief was cut from the "omnibus" bill in a hard bargain with Republicans. In a flash, she replied, "You're telling Noah about the flood."

Pelosi is often painted as a coastal elitist, but learned her political lessons in working-class Baltimore, where her father was mayor.

The huge omnibus bill passed the House late that night. Then it was up to Philadelphia for a party issues retreat. Groggy members slept on buses.

After a visit to Independence Hall, Pelosi introduced President Joe Biden with sober praise. "These are times that try (our) souls," she echoed Revolutionary thinker Thomas Paine.

Nodding to nerves about messaging the midterm election, Pelosi said, "We have to show the public the relationship between democracy and their kitchen table concerns."

It's no secret their slim majority is at stake.

A keen savvy was on display at a New York event.

Monday morning saw Pelosi at Brooklyn Bridge Park with Caucus Chair, Hakeem Jeffries, speaking on better bridges, roads and rail on the way from Washington.

Blunt and effective, 51-year-old Jeffries is the likely contender to succeed — or challenge — Pelosi as speaker. He quoted "Hamilton" in one Trump impeachment trial.

Wednesday was the historic joint address to Congress by Volodymyr Zelenskyy, president of battered and bombed Ukraine. Pelosi co-hosted an hour that shook Congress to the core.

Pelosi framed Russian President Vladimir Putin's war as an assault on all democracy. "Slava Ukraini!"

Then came St. Patrick's Day. Her lunch for the Irish prime minister went on — despite his absence due to COVID-19.

Pelosi gave a Champagne toast and invited a Riverdance performance that crossed party lines, sheer cheer in troubled times. Exhilarating.

All: women won the vote in 1920.

Three Stages of Violence: Hollywood, Washington, Ukraine

March 30, 2022

Hollywood. Washington. Ukraine.

Violence is breaking out all over, in places we thought we'd never see it: on the Academy Awards stage, in the Capitol and a war in Europe.

Are these ugly events somehow connected?

Let's take the Academy scene first. Will Smith struck Chris Rock across the face. The scene seemed out of a movie. In an earlier era, there would have been a duel when the next day dawned.

Alexander Hamilton got caught in the gentlemen's "honor" code in 1804, when he lost his life in a duel for trash-talking Aaron Burr.

Rock made a cruel jest from the stage, mocking Jada Pinkett Smith's painful medical condition that caused her hair loss. Her face contorted and, in a split second, her actor husband rushed Rock in a rage and hit him hard.

Alopecia is no joke, as a congresswoman of color, Ayanna Pressley, D-Mass., revealed. A traumatic and public illness, it feels like losing a part of you.

Still, Smith's violence and cursing upstaged everything in the lackluster Oscars show. He wept as he won the Best Actor award, again in a scene that seemed scripted, hard to watch.

The assault was unacceptable, considered a crime. But insulting and humiliating a woman in public, in front of millions, is just a misdemeanor—I know, right?

Chivalry is not dead, encoded in our genes. Smith acted from an ancient desire to defend his wife. Even if understandable, his scenes were way over the line in our times.

Here in our town, we're grappling with violence on democracy itself.

The Jan. 6 mob assault on the Capitol is a wound wide

open to investigation. The House Select Committee has interviewed hundreds of witnesses to set up hearings on the conspiracy to undo the peaceful transfer of power.

A coup in the Capitol is what we narrowly avoided that dark day descending into night.

Former President Donald Trump was involved, "more likely than not," a federal judge stated Monday, in a corrupt plot to steal the Electoral Count that certified Joe Biden as the winner.

Never before in history had a presidential loser violently challenged the election results — which weren't even close in 2020.

President George Washington, a hero and general, could have stayed in power if he chose, but rather stepped down in peace.

The first president set the precedent in 1797. We lost the plot in the winter of 2021.

I know for a fact that witnesses still struggle with memories of the siege, because I was there. The bloodshed of 150 police officers defended the lives of lawmakers, who fled. It was not a pretty picture for the world.

When we thought we were beyond shock, came the news the wife of Supreme Court Justice Clarence Thomas, Ginni, sought to keep Trump in power after he lost. Her email trail with the White House chief of staff, Mark Meadows, is all raw partisanship.

In a first, Mrs. Thomas may be invited to testify before the committee. Meadows was voted in criminal contempt of Congress for refusing to appear. Chairman Bennie Thompson, D-Miss., is running a swift ship.

Then there's the Russian war on Ukraine. The brazen aggression of President Vladimir Putin was hard to believe. Sure enough, he crossed the line. Ukraine President Volodymyr Zelenskyy, a former actor, grabbed the world stage in the weeks since.

Shattering scenes from Ukraine cities and civilians woke

up Western democracies allied in NATO. Yes, Virginia, a war could happen again in Europe after two world wars.

Actor Sean Penn, pleading from Poland, urged the Academy to let Zelenskyy address the audience on Oscar night by video, as the leader had done to a somber Congress.

Zelenskyy's bravery and clarion call could have calmed the tempest, putting the Rock-Smith imbroglio into perspective.

If this war ends with Ukraine independent of Russia and NATO, (like Finland) that would be the best achievable peace. The tragic irony is that this might have been hammered out before the bombs began falling.

The old rules of engagement are not working for our brutal new world. Will Smith showed some remorse.

The worst actors in the world, Trump and Putin, would never do that.

April Brings Uncertain Things, Now and Then

April 20, 2022

WASHINGTON — Dear April, national poetry month, are you the cruelest month? The first line of "The Waste Land" says so, and poet T.S. Eliot wrote it 100 years ago, 1922.

So, 2022, let's look at you.

Spring snow after joyful opening days at baseball parks celebrating Dodger great Jackie Robinson isn't a good sign. Gardens are thrown off the seasons after a long winter.

But the worst of it is raging many thousands of miles away, in a conflict that burst into the open. Russian President Vladimir Putin's ruthless near-conquest of eastern Ukraine, the Donbas, is on. That region may soon fall.

At the rare convergence of Easter, Passover and Ramadan this April, some people prayed that peace would break out in Russia's war on Ukraine. One was Pope Francis, who pleaded for an Easter truce.

"We have seen all too much blood, too much violence," Francis declared, noting the suffering in several shattered cities.

Rome fell on deaf ears.

When the war is over, it will take years to pick up the pieces, no matter which side wins. Ukraine s civilian casualties are mounting, each life irreplaceable. That toll will be on the world's conscience for much time to come.

Ukraine President Volodymyr Zelenskyy's stirring moments of bravery and unlikely glory — missiles sinking a Russian warship — may make him a tragic hero in the end.

Beautiful and bittersweet, April won't tell yet.

Meanwhile, we Americans endure the hardship of higher gas prices as we fill up our SUV tanks. Pollsters predict that inflation will be the bane of President Joe Biden's existence in a November blowout in the midterm elections.

With a slight Democratic majority in both chambers, Congress could easily change hands.

But much more than gas prices is at stake.

Weary Americans are on the knife-edge between saying the pandemic is over and fearing its return to take more lives. The loss of one million to the coronavirus echoes the deadly influenza epidemic of 1918, which spread after the First World War.

Those ghastly events colored the pessimistic prism of Eliot's masterpiece poem.

Perhaps you know a friend or family member who was so careful about COVID-19 for two years and suddenly caught it this April. There is no clear consensus on the pandemic, which mirrors the deep cut in our body politic.

Public places, planes and trains are now opening up without mask mandates. We can only hope that a Donald Trump-appointed judge (who struck down travel mask mandates) knows better than public health experts.

The hatred on the faces of the white Trump mob who attacked the Capitol on Jan. 6, 2021, was telling and fearful. Thousands came from every corner of the country in the pandemic. One in five were military veterans.

At the loser's invitation ("will be wild") they aimed to disrupt democracy's unbroken custom of counting the 2020 Electoral College votes.

The pandemic also saw a sharp rise in pedestrian deaths, homicides and suicides across America. Therapists work overtime to treat anxiety and depression.

Introverts first thought Zoom answered their prayers. Extroverts and live performers wept with loneliness. Children missed their friends and a chunk of their childhood. Confinement does not agree with the American spirit, I know, right?

Our soul is at stake. We were never meant to be timid, the nation that conquered the frontier, won world wars and flew to the moon.

Simply put, this health crisis did not bring out the best in us, utterly lacking in unity. Most found that our private spheres and families could not fill our longing for the free public square.

April come she will, but will that fraught feeling of fear go?

(If Elon Musk takes social media's throne, will he let the loser pretender back on Twitter?)

The cruelest April day in memory was when Martin Luther King Jr. was murdered. Presidents Franklin D. Roosevelt and Abraham Lincoln, both beloved, died in April.

To be fair, bards also praise April as a muse of history and love.

Remember the midnight ride of Paul Revere ("Listen, my children, and you shall hear") by Henry Wadsworth Longfellow.

Said Shakespeare: "O! how this spring of love resembleth/the uncertain glory of an April day."

Key word: uncertain.

How Far the Party Fell Into the Abyss: From Hatch to McCarthy

April 27, 2022

WASHINGTON — The Hon. Orrin Hatch, a staunchly conservative Republican senator from Utah, is no longer with us. He died in Salt Lake City at 88. Hatch's seven terms in the Senate are a record, and it's fair to say time changed him into a better man.

Kevin McCarthy, the House Republican Leader, is the perfect foil for Hatch. At 57, the vapid Californian struts through the House like it's a fraternity, with white male "bros."

McCarthy often whines about "Pelosi," belittling House Speaker Nancy Pelosi, the California Democrat.

Insincere about all but his lust to become house speaker, McCarthy denied — lied about — his resolve to tell former President Donald Trump to resign after the Jan. 6, 2021, mob attack on the Capitol.

Remember the days when getting caught lying on tape was a problem? Now, contradicting oneself is a minor hiccup in a news cycle.

Contrasting Hatch and McCarthy shows us how far the Republican party fell in one political lifetime — or generation.

On his way down into the ashpit, McCarthy makes Senate Republican Leader Mitch McConnell, Ky., look steady in his stance against Trump.

From rookie reporting days, I have a personal memory of Hatch inviting me to listen to some country gospel songs he composed. His smile lit up the office. I had to revise my opinion of him upward.

As much as liberals disagreed with Hatch, we liked and respected his warm humanity and Mormon faith. He arrived in Washington, vowing to take on everything Sen. Edward Kennedy, D-Mass., championed. In the end, they became best of friends.

McCarthy is not an honorable man like Hatch.

Charm has pretty much left the Republican Party.

Unlike the Kennedy-Hatch friendship, which led to bipartisan laws, the McCarthy-Trump alliance reveals how hollow McCarthy was in pursuing power and the outgoing Trump's favor.

There was no low to which McCarthy would not go to hold onto his raucous caucus, which suddenly included Georgia's own Rep. Marjorie Taylor Greene on Jan. 3, 2021. Unofficially the biggest mouth of Trump in the House, Greene called for "Marshall law" in that fateful January.

Anyone who was in the House chamber on the darkest day—as McCarthy was, as I was—knew the bloodthirsty mob almost broke in. Over the sound of gunfire, we—the members and the press—narrowly escaped from the siege's fury.

The shock was fresh when McCarthy spoke something close to the truth. He condemned mob violence in a floor speech and later admitted Trump bore some responsibility. He told colleagues he'd advise Trump to resign, even with President Joe Biden about to be sworn into office.

In a call with Trump as the attack raged, McCarthy urged Trump to call the armed mob off.

Good for McCarthy in one desperate moment. Trump taunted "Kevin," saying the pro-Trump thousands were more upset about the election than he was.

Within weeks, McCarthy visited Mara-a-Lago to publicly patch things up with Trump.

Quavering McCarthy gave Trump the power he craved. If he'd treated Trump like a pariah, a pretender or an enemy of the Constitution, that might have stuck. But he sold his own soul for free.

McCarthy's vote against Trump's impeachment over the Jan. 6 violence clinched the devil's deal. His lack of leadership limits let loose a volcano of Trumpian trash talk.

The new rules were that there were no rules among roughly 200 House Republicans. Only 10 voted to impeach

Trump, including Liz Cheney, R-Wyo.

Freshmen Republicans Greene, Lauren Boebert, Colo., and Madison Cawthorn, N.C., poisoned the well further into a partisan firestorm.

Don't get me wrong. Specific things Hatch did — in 1991, in 2017 — I can't accept. Shouldering the elephantine Trump tax bill, giving massive breaks to the rich, stands out.

But it helps to have some love lost between the party aisle. For Hatch and Kennedy, their friendship resulted in laws helping AIDS patients and health insurance for the working poor.

The straight-laced Mormon helped the liberal lion beat his drinking problem.

Journalists enjoyed lighter moments that now seem so much scarcer. A reporter friend once showed Hatch the Beethoven piano sonata sheets (in F minor) he was learning.

"Why don't you try something a bit tougher?" Hatch said.

A Sad Situation, the State of the Nation

May 18, 2022

WASHINGTON — Ineffable. The state and soul of the nation is just that. The National Cathedral bell tolls for thee and me.

But all I have are words. Let me try to explain the sharp sense of loss we carry these days. The fear is real, that the worst of us are stealing America's meaning from the rest of us.

At once, we're suffering four crises: race hatred, human rights, public health and democracy itself.

Buffalo, New York, is a fine city that was bloodied, with 10 shot dead, from an armed young hater who drove 200 miles to hunt prey in a Black neighborhood grocery store. A quotidian afternoon. He showed no mercy to the dignity of those humans, old or young.

They are gone, but the shock of such racial violence shakes the city and country for a long time to come. The grief will never go away for their friends and families. The violation to public square peace is ineffable.

Thank you, fork-tongued fox Tucker Carlson, for your white nationalist "replacement" theory. You're our own Imperial Klan wizard, hidden well under your veneer.

Merchants of hate sell these days, especially online, but the FBI is flat-footed on an internet that's as wild as the Old West.

On a second front, reproductive rights are human rights that go beyond one's body. They mean a woman or girl's dignity — and yes, her life, liberty and pursuit of happiness. Life chances are bound up with reproductive freedom.

That's the law of the land for 50 years. Yet five radical Right Supreme Court members think they can take that away from us. Just like that. And maybe they will, because they can. Most of the nine justices are conservative Catholics.

You tell me, is Rome coming home for us, into our

intimate spaces?

The Supreme Court is meant to expand human rights as time goes along. That's the march of progress and the optimist's view of history. But hear me now, if the Court were to strip away rights from a whole class of people, it would be us — women and girls.

You can count on it.

I heard the bell tolling the day in May when coronavirus deaths reached one million — two years and two months since the pandemic began. Again, our faith in America's spirit and can-do capability was tested and failed. I know, right?

Haphazard was the word for government handling of the crisis. Former President Donald Trump somehow managed to polarize the nation on wearing masks. His talent for sowing seeds of anger among us, even as hundreds were dying every day, is absolutely unmatched. Give him that.

Once COVID-19 vaccines were available and President Joe Biden took office, reason prevailed. Still, so many were lonely, scared or sick.

The children who stayed home from school were socially and educationally starved during the pandemic. Lots of chance meetings, conversations and friendships never got off the ground. A favorite clothing boutique closed. The sidewalks were eerily empty.

Time stood still yet passed, leaving us sadder if not wiser. Missing one million people from our lives became a silent shared burden of sorrow.

One last component of crisis: Democracy came under siege when a mob of tens of thousands rushed the Capitol walls on Jan. 6, 2021. They aimed to undo the peaceful transfer of power for the very first time.

Trump invited and incited them in the light of day. The Proud Boys and the Oath Keepers, among other extremist groups, answered his call. They came from as far away as Texas and California. They posted travel plans on the internet.

In the darkness before dawn, Biden emerged as the

winner, after deadly attacks on the Capitol. I was there, inside. All we knew at the teary end was that American democracy had a very close call.

Part of our present predicament goes back to Roger Taney, whose bust is buried in the bowels of the Capitol. As chief justice in 1857, he enshrined white supremacy into law with his infamous Dred Scott decision, ruling Black people could never have rights as citizens.

The cruel, political Taney court led straight to the Civil War. Clearly, he haunts us to this day—ineffably.

Midterms: The First Stress Test for Democracy (And Trump) Since Jan. 6

May 25, 2022

Today is Tuesday, democracy's favorite day. There's a lot to talk about in that word.

Primaries are upon us. The national news media, especially The Washington Post, can't get the story straight about former President Donald Trump's sway in the midterms.

Barely a week ago, Trump's "potency" was front-page news, to be feared by all Republicans that faced voters without his favor.

Now, not so much.

Georgia Gov. Brian Kemp, a Republican who openly defied Trump, will almost surely defeat former Sen. David Perdue, Trump's hand-picked man.

Trump sought revenge on Kemp for not playing along with the plot to undo the 2020 presidential election results.

All Republican candidates ought to take a page from Kemp's honest courage as he prevails over a revenge-obsessed former president.

Let Trump bask in the humiliation of that Georgia rebuke. Salt in the wound was former Vice President Mike Pence campaigning for Kemp.

Trump didn't fare well in a North Carolina race, either.

His young pet and hell-on-wheels congressman, Rep. Madison Cawthorn, lost his reelection bid. The House gave a sigh of relief, because Cawthorn carried a loaded gun around airports. His mouth was just as dangerous.

Dr. Mehmet Oz, whom Trump endorsed in the Pennsylvania Senate race, did not win outright. The oleaginous Oz is locked in a recount, though Trump suggested he just declare victory.

Oh, don't you miss that flagrant disrespect for fairness and the rule of law? Even if Oz wins the primary, the smart money is on Democratic Lt. Gov. John Fetterman, with an appealing, authentic and dressed-down persona.

Also in Pennsylvania, a Trump loyalist, Doug Mastriano is the Republican nominee for governor. He marched with the Jan. 6 mob. He appears too extreme for the land of my birthplace and Quaker state founded on William Penn's brotherly love. Josh Shapiro, the state attorney general, is a safer bet.

Even in Ohio, getting redder every year, the same pattern could hold true. Trump endorsed JD Vance, the brash bestselling author of "Hillbilly Elegy," for an open Senate seat. He won the primary.

Yet Rep. Tim Ryan, D-Ohio, son of Youngstown with a flair for heartfelt oratory, will wear well with statewide voters. He's the real deal. That seat could be a critical Democratic pickup.

The press fell for Trump's grandiose claims—lies—too many times, giving him "free media" and more power than he possessed. It's another insidious kind of inflation.

So, the Post had to backtrack and note Republican governors are finding that Trump's support isn't worth much. It's more of an illusion, or a delusion.

Fancy how sweet, not to hear or read another word about Trump's power in the midterm elections. The emperor of dangerous nonsense had his day, my friends in the press corps.

Set thyselves free, the great Quaker governor might say to reporters who just can't quit Trump. Penn was a brilliant Founding Father.

American democracy never had such a bad sport before. The Capitol was sacked by the British in wartime. But it was never attacked by a war within, tens of thousands of Americans in an attack that disrupted the constitutional transfer of power.

Inside, it felt like the Roman siege of the Temple in Jerusalem. We did not know how the day would end.

What we knew: Angry white supremacists were incited and invited to break into the Capitol by a president. Sedition—

no more, no less.

The importance of the first election since that dark January day can't be overstated. It's a stress test for the body politic's health.

So, it must be fair and square, after faith in our age-old system was shaken in front of our faces. It's an imperative to show that we can meet at the polls as peaceable citizens.

Speaking of that, the Greek prime minister gave a rousing address to Congress, invited by House Speaker Nancy Pelosi, D-Calif. Democracy, invented in ancient Greece, "remains the most profound leap of faith in human history," declared Kyriakos Mitsotakis.

Authoritarianism is now testing its strength, he added.

Pelosi clearly thought the divided House needed a refresher of what it's all about.

On 2022 Tuesdays, let the best men and women win. Trump's proxies must be defeated and done.

Sharing a Cell in History Hell: Trump and Nixon

June 8, 2022

WASHINGTON — Former Presidents Donald Trump and Richard Nixon share a cell in presidential history hell.

Their arc is apt, 50 years apart, from June 1972 to June 2022. No matter how much time they do down there, the damage their deeds did to American democracy lives long after them.

Trump and Nixon, first-class haters who viewed the world through an "enemies" prism, especially the press, sat at the center of conspiracies to hold onto power at all costs.

They were ruthless destroyers of the dream that Abraham Lincoln called "the last best hope of earth."

If Nixon's 1972 Watergate tale disillusioned a generation of children like me, with lost faith in government, think what Trump's barrage of trash-talking tweets, lies, insults and boasts has done to children on his watch — or children watching him.

The first 12 years of my father's life were with President Franklin D. Roosevelt, a jaunty voice and trusted leader in a world war and Depression.

Presidents matter, for better or worse — or worst.

On Thursday night live, the magnitude of the Jan. 6, 2021, attack on the Capitol will unfold for the first time, in a House Select Committee hearing.

This town is on edge about reliving the Capitol crime committed in broad daylight. It's still the stuff of nightmares for some witnesses.

Incited and invited by the president, a mob of 10,000 stormed our marble beacon, aiming to hold Congress captive and disrupt the ritual of certifying the presidential election.

Never before has the peaceful transfer of power come under deadly siege. The Trump mob had a list of who they wanted. First: Vice President Mike Pence, the only one of the president's men who defied the scheme to steal the election.

Pence's handsome head was in grave danger. Trump also wanted revenge on House Speaker Nancy Pelosi, the only leader who ever confronted him to his face, ripped up a speech and led an impeachment (on Ukraine.)

Jan. 6 was carefully chosen.

Trump knew lawmakers would be fully present in the House and Senate chambers that date, chosen by the Constitution. With Inauguration Day two weeks away, it was his last chance. He invited supporters to travel here. The word spread among his base with lightning speed.

The Proud Boys and other extremist groups made travel, hotel and weapons plans openly on the internet. They made no secret of their plans, but the FBI missed the plot. Again. Another massive intelligence failure, this one on their doorstep.

You wonder what they do all day.

Proud Boys leaders were just charged with seditious conspiracy.

At the same time, we look back on the June night Watergate break-in and burglary, a crime ordered by the Nixon White House to penetrate the Democratic National Committee.

Some suspected from the start that the coverup led straight to the top. But Nixon refused to give way until he finally resigned under pressure from his party on Aug. 8, 1974.

For once, Nixon spoke a knowing truth to the American people that last day: "Those who hate you don't win unless you hate them, and then you destroy yourself."

I remember my father telling me the Watergate news when he picked me up from tennis.

I remember young John Dean testifying, looking innocent when he wasn't so innocent, as the White House counsel. On a new CNN series, he seems a wise elder, but ambition and pressure took him down the wrong road to prison.

The best quote came from former aide Alexander

Butterfield: Nixon never thought of telling the truth. Butterfield spilled the beans that Nixon taped himself.

Long story short, a Watergate security guard detected tape on the DNC door, which led to a president's fall.

That's quaint next to a raging mass that caused 150 police casualties. If not for the 800 city police officers who saved the day, the blood on the building—and Trump's hands—would never be washed clean.

Rep. Liz Cheney, a Wyoming Republican, noted Trump has shown no "remorse."

Really, Liz? Trump doesn't know the meaning of the word.

Trump spoke of "American carnage" in his inaugural speech facing the National Mall, which captured the tragic end of his four years: another American arc.

Athens and America: Helpful Hints for the Fix We're In

June 22, 2022

ATHENS, GREECE—Greetings from the land where democracy began 2,500 years ago.

I came seeking shelter under the Aegean sun from American democracy running ragged.

Our own government is the oldest extant democracy in the world. But America is reeling from the revelations of the House select committee hearings on the Jan. 6 mob attack on the Capitol. I witnessed the siege from inside the walls and covered two somber committee hearings.

So far, it's clear our worst fears about former President Donald Trump's ruthless scheme to steal his lost election are true, and then some.

So, I have some helpful hints from here to send home.

The most important takeaway from Athens is how precious, rare and fragile democracy is. Its backstory is a timely cautionary tale. My urgent message on the winds Odysseus sailed is simple: We must cherish what Americans take for granted.

Trump's violent conspiracy to hold onto power was indeed like a Greek drama. The Proud Boys were the tragic chorus, along with calls to hang Vice President Mike Pence—the hero who saved the day. Believe me, the mob would have done it. They had a list of who they wanted.

We who witnessed the un-American, murderous sound and fury knew who sent the mob of 30,000 that winter afternoon. And we knew without committee hearings. Only one man had the hubris and the power to dare to do that.

The majesty of the gleaming Parthenon towering over the city is so much more than an art history book can say. We walked up high to behold the place where the greatest philosophers met in dialogue, leaders gave orations and where

Greeks worshiped their gods.

Even more crucial, this is where democracy was first practiced. The radical idea was that each citizen of Athens was the equal of any other. Fancy that.

The citizen was the essence of governing the "city-state" in the 5th century B.C. This period was the Athenian golden age. American revolutionaries had much the same idea in 1776, inspired by Athens. One man, one vote.

America and Athens shared a tragic flaw: each excluded women and enslaved people from being citizens. In our case, the slave-owning South pressured the nation's founders and won greater representation in Congress. While denied all rights, people who were enslaved still counted as 3/5 of a person.

Confederate state Texas also forgot to tell some emancipated people they were free until a Union general rode to proclaim their freedom on June 19, 1865. Texas was two and a half years late for President Abraham Lincoln's chosen date of Jan. 1, 1863.

In ancient Athens, the principle of majority representation and rule was established. In our Constitution, strangely, the minority wins more often than you might think. Take this: all three recent Supreme Court appointments were made by a president (Trump) who lost the popular vote.

If a political leader was turning into a tyrant, Athenians invented a way to get rid of him. He was ostracized by the people of the city. The results of "ostraka" were likely more direct and swifter than Trump's two impeachment trials.

Athens is a fabulous place to be glad you're alive, bubbling over with beautiful everything: literal layers of the past, sculptural art, architecture, ideas and Homeric poetry even older than the city's heyday.

At the peak of its power, Athens was the envy and glory of the world. Her warships rode the waves, feared by allies and rivals alike.

Sound familiar?

But that did not last long, about a half-century. The long Peloponnesian War with Sparta depleted its treasury and a generation of young men. Athenian dominance and democracy ebbed in the ancient world, and the city was conquered more than once.

The leading light went out of the classical world, though Rome and other conquerors treated Athens with respect for its cultural place.

Our democracy is under threat, under siege, right now. The most public expression of that festering "war within" waged by extremists took place on Jan. 6, 2021. The November 2022 midterms are the next showdown.

The forces opposing democracy could crush our fondest hopes and dreams for the future. The proud Greek past is telling us that.

A Pearl of Hope For An Unhappy Birthday

July 6, 2022

Some birthdays are better or worse than others. America's 246th was a lot like 1863.

In a dark gloom, a civil war without cannons is now on, full blast.

On one side, we have a relentless truth-seeking missile, the Jan. 6 committee. I was in the stately room when Cassidy Hutchinson testified that former President Donald Trump lunged at a Secret Service agent because he wanted to direct his coup, literally, every step of the way to the Capitol.

The hearing was jaw-dropping, even for the press. Through Hutchinson's crystal calm words, it became clear beyond doubt the armed mob assembled to seize the election for Trump with force and blood. They came at his beck and call. Its sound and fury was astounding, about 30,000 strong.

I was in the Capitol when the House chamber was under siege. Even now, I can scarcely stand viewing the gruesome attack on democracy's citadel.

On the other side, the Supreme Court just declared war on the American people. Five men and one woman, to be exact, showed no restraint in lashes on common sense, law and custom in the public square.

It's not enough to take 50 years of human rights away from women and young girls. All six Republicans also lifted gun restrictions and environmental regulation of carbon emissions. Then they skipped town.

This comes as July 4 marks another mass shooting, in Highland Park, Illinois, as the parade was about to begin.

The Trump trifecta on the court is cold enough: Neil Gorsuch, Brett Kavanaugh and Amy Coney Barrett, who took the late Justice Ruth Bader Ginsburg's place on the bench days before the election, no tears.

But it's the petulant senior Republicans, Samuel Alito

and Clarence Thomas, who bear the blame for this hard right turn against the will of the American people.

Chief Justice John Roberts, who puts on a show of being centrist, can be counted as a confederate in this war.

After all, he favored dark money as free speech and led striking down parts of the Voting Rights Act.

Now Roberts has sided against women and girls, gun safety and action on climate change, like the rest of the Republican supermajority. He can't coast anymore with his polished manners.

What's more, Roberts was named by George W. Bush, who lost the popular vote. He has no connection with "we the people." The same is true for Alito and the new Trump wing.

Being linked with unpopular presidents further undercuts their authority to sit in judgment on us. And it makes it harder to accept their harsh decisions.

If you don't believe me about the crisis of confidence in the Supreme Court, author Norman Ornstein, the leading expert on Washington politics, had this to say:

"Since the Civil War, we have not had anything as dangerous as what we face now. The Supreme Court has gone completely rogue and cannot be trusted to protect our constitutional framework.

"Too much of the public is simply unaware of the danger. And chillingly, many don't really care."

A pending case on state legislatures overseeing federal elections is also truly alarming, Ornstein says.

Let me tell you about my Fourth. I went down to the National Mall to be inspired by the Folklife Festival. Under the hot sun I spied the Smithsonian partnership this year: the United Arab Emirates.

A curious choice, given our democracy needs a helping hand.

Yet here's a pearl of hope that never fails on the Fourth. Gen. Robert E. Lee, daring and reckless, led his Confederate army farther North than ever into Pennsylvania.

(Compare that move to the brazen Supreme Court.)

The Confederate army clashed with a huge Union army. The mighty battles they fought in the Devil's Den, the Peach Orchard and finally, in vain, Pickett's Charge, took place on July 1, 2 and 3.

Then the smoke cleared, cannons fell silent and casualties were strewn all over beautiful farmland.

Lee lost the turning point of the Civil War by the Fourth of July, 1863. The Union won the midway battle under Gen. George Meade.

On July 4, 1863, the Civil War was ours to lose.

But it was—and is—a close call.

Trump's Knots and Dots: It's All Over

July 20, 2022

A figurative noose is tightening around Donald Trump's neck.

The sweet thing is that he knows it. The desperado is shrewd enough to sense his day is done.

Let's count the knots. Some are political, some are legal.

We already know the dots add up to a portrait of a screaming, swearing president who tried to overthrow the government by force.

The crackerjack House select committee on the mob attack on the Capitol is tying Trumpian knots in public opinion. Hearing by hearing, witness by witness, they're telling a sordid story nobody could make up. Thursday in primetime will conclude the best summer true crime story ever.

I mean the noose of justice, of course, not a noose and gallows, which Trump's armed mob brought to "Hang Mike Pence" at the Capitol riot on Jan. 6, 2021. Trump's vice president was in grave danger that day.

The tables have turned.

In real time, Trump suggested Pence might "deserve" it. For Pence refused to play his part in the violent conspiracy to hold onto presidential power — the first such plot in American history.

Like a Roman emperor, Trump fell under a depraved spell at the crowd size. The 30,000 marching to storm the Capitol thrilled him.

As promised, the deadly scene was "wild" when vast throngs crawled up terrace steps and walls, broke glass on marble floors and rushed the chambers of Congress. The House and Senate were in, certifying the winner of the 2020 election in a constitutional ritual.

In a long day's journey after midnight, the winner was Joseph Biden.

Now Trump's political hold is waning, with a few chosen candidates losing.

Nearly half of Republican primary voters oppose Trump running for a second term, a New York Times poll found. After all, he lost the popular vote twice, in 2016 and 2020.

Even among his sheeplike Republican supporters, "Vote to Keep Me Out of Prison" is a loser's slogan. Come a year from now, fresh blood will sell better than a mean old man. His party may flock to a mean young man, Florida Republican Gov. Ron DeSantis.

Frankly, a lust for revenge and a wish to escape the noose of justice won't play to the wider American public, exhausted by Trump's four years of fecklessness in office.

If you look at the legal jeopardy Trump faces, it's no wonder why he wants to run early for president in the 2024 election and escape the law behind the White House walls.

Looming on the horizon is a criminal case. In Georgia, a special grand jury is investigating whether Trump and allies tried to undo the 2020 election result. Biden won the state.

Trump directly called a Georgia official to tell him the exact margin of victory he needed: 11,780 votes. Brazen is his brand. He applied the same brutal scheming to democracy that he used in business—and it almost worked.

The Republican governor, Brian Kemp, made an enemy out of Trump by not backing him up. Kemp won reelection easily.

In New York, Trump is in rising waters for his business practices, especially in taxation. (That's how authorities got Al Capone.) A civil case is pending, brought by the state attorney general for possible fraudulent reporting on the value of buildings and golf courses.

To pile on, Steve Bannon, a top Trump strategist, is on trial for criminal contempt of Congress.

Author of the crude "American carnage" line in Trump's inaugural speech, Bannon finally agreed to appear before the House select committee.

An extremist, Bannon unbound is a bad look for Trump.

The Justice Department, spurred by the evidence and hard work of the House committee, may just act. Wouldn't that be boffo, Attorney General Merrick Garland?

Indicting Trump for a seditious plot is the decisive act — or knot — in our tragic drama of democracy.

In fact, it's emerged that only the threat of a mass resignation of Justice lawyers kept Trump from appointing a loyalist, Jeffrey Clark, as attorney general to put his planned coup in place.

Chances are, Trump knows the jig is up. He'll never go quietly into the darkness before the dawn. But his day is done.

Jamie Stiehm

A Midsummer's Nightmare: Onstage in Washington

July 27, 2022

While Washington burns, enchanted evening relief from hot air floats from the Folger Theatre's "A Midsummer Night's Dream."

In real midsummer 2022, we're caught in an agonizing Greek drama, with a Shakespearean villain. Some leading scenes and characters follow.

(Advisory: avoid choking on your morning coffee.)

Young and somber, Cassidy Hutchinson is like mythical Cassandra. She spoke in slow, rhythmic cadences telling the truth about the offstage sound and fury of former President Donald Trump, before and during the Jan. 6 Capitol riot.

An agape world heard her testimony in a Jan. 6 House select committee hearing on the Capitol storming by a massive armed mob.

The witness inside the White House West Wing that day, as an aide, hit the pitch-perfect note: "Un-American."

We could see Trump's porcelain plate of lunch thrown, with bloodlike ketchup trickling down the lovely White House walls.

Oh yes, he's American Macbeth. Central casting.

The election loser, Trump was murderous in plotting against any leader in his way to more power. Vice President Mike Pence, whom the mob hunted, was first on his list.

Then came the five-alarm reveal that Trump really, really wanted to lead the mob march to the Capitol after his speech inciting the tens of thousands.

As Hutchinson told it, Trump lunged at a Secret Service agent driving him to the White House, so desperate was he to go to the Capitol to confront and disrupt Congress.

The marble temple was full of lawmakers, certifying the election.

The stage was set for a coup.

As a sage editor noted, if that one driver gave into the raging Trump, we might be in a very different place right now.

American democracy almost fell into a demagogue's hands.

Cassandra's fate as a truth-teller was that nobody believed her. However, Hutchinson's tale rang as all too true.

Even their names, Cassandra and Cassidy, echo across time.

In the prime-time hearing, members of Congress sat still and wiped tears from their eyes as they heard how Trump refused to call off the deadly mob for three hours — "187 minutes" was the Greek chorus.

They heard gunshots inside the Capitol — so did I — and cries coming closer to their chambers. They feared for their lives.

In the dust of the Supreme Court's decision to strike down reproductive rights in Roe v. Wade, the House Republicans crept one step farther into your most private lives.

Maybe we should all know this chilling fact, in case the radical Republicans soon take over the blue House.

In the raucous chamber, I watched a floor vote on the human right to contraception. Nearly 200 House Republicans oppose contraception, now on record. So they say.

What they do in their private lives, who knows? Honestly, who cares?

My question: Have they read "Lysistrata?"

Meanwhile, in a courthouse near the Capitol, a top Trump strategist, Steve Bannon, was on trial. Scruffy and defiant on the sidewalk, a minor player, he pledged allegiance to Trump.

The night before Jan. 6, he declared, "All hell is going to break loose."

But Bannon refused to speak to the select committee at all and never took the stand.

The jury found him guilty of criminal contempt for

Congress.

The judge, Carl J. Nichols, was named by Trump, a piquant twist. Bannon's appeal and sentence remain to be seen.

House Republicans did better on gay marriage, another vote Speaker Nancy Pelosi, D-Calif., smartly pressed to the floor. Election season is in the air. Only 157 opposed it. Call it progress.

Seventeen Democratic House members got arrested under the hot sun near the Supreme Court, protesting the Roe v. Wade overturn.

"Like coming home," Rep. Barbara Lee, D-Calif., said of the rights protest, citing the late civil rights hero John Lewis' motto of getting in "Good Trouble."

Rep. Jackie Speier, also a California Democrat, organized the demonstration. Nobody went to jail. Sixteen women and only one man, Michigan's Rep. Andy Levin, got into the act.

Why this tragic flaw?

"Ask them," Lee replied, meaning about 130 men in the caucus.

Democrats must show a better ensemble to win under the sun and against the winds.

Field Notes: The Summer Burn Of '22

Aug. 24, 2022

The scorching summer of '22 may be one we never forget, as a turning point in the wheels of weather and politics.

As August closes, the cicadas still sing, but they won't for long. Black-eyed Susan flowers have just their black eyes left. Summer's lease is almost over.

And this country has changed, sobered since the pandemic hit.

First, we lost reproductive rights in late June.

Between floods in the South, drought in New England, wildfires in the West and hurricane season on the way, climate change is hitting home. Literally.

Or, should I say, climate crisis.

Lake Powell running dry is a water crisis for seven states. An awakening that Mother Nature is fragile—and angry—is at hand. The wisdom of building cities in the desert around the automobile was flawed.

In August, Congress took serious action on climate for the very first time. Or should I say, Democrats in Congress acted to cut carbon emissions in the Inflation Reduction Act. The Senate passed the legislation 51-50 with zero Republican votes. Fie!

President Joe Biden signed the monumental bill into law, a boost to his political fortunes. That's "luck of the Irish" for the president, who could not press Congress to pass a similar bill last summer.

Actually, Senate Majority Leader Chuck Schumer, D-N.Y., deserves credit for the deal. Biden had COVID-19 at the time. Schumer met with Sen. Joe Manchin, D-W. Va., in secret to bring his entire caucus of 50 Democrats together.

So thrilled were they to break through the climate wall that Democrats shared the spoils of victory.

Sagging in approval ratings, Biden needed a big win this

summer. Just like he needed a bare majority to hold onto the Senate. Just like he needed to win the South Carolina primary in 2020 to stay in the race.

Remember? Biden came back from behind, again and again, the winds blowing his way.

Now Democrats have a landmark to write home about for the fall midterms. Pundits predicted the election would be a Republican sweep. Now they're not so sure.

Even shrewd Mitch McConnell, Senate Republican Leader, R-Ky., agrees with me that the Senate will likely remain blue.

With strong candidates like Rep. Tim Ryan and Lt. Gov. John Fetterman in Ohio and Pennsylvania, running against J.D. Vance and Dr. Mehmet Oz, Democrats could pick up open seats.

Vance and Oz are weak; they've never faced voters before. There's an art to campaigning and connecting with commoners at the state fair. It helps to be likable, but the celebrity author and doctor come across as spoiled elites.

Republican Sens. Ron Johnson of Wisconsin and Marco Rubio of Florida are vulnerable, with strong challengers in Lt. Gov. Mandela Barnes and Rep. Val Demings.

A former police chief, Demings starred on the House team of impeachment managers the first time former President Donald Trump was on trial in the Senate.

Oh, yeah — the criminally insane gale-force human hurricane.

Inescapably, the 45th president can't leave us in peace. There's no end in sight to his dirty deeds after the latest: The FBI searched his Florida mansion for classified state secrets he stole from the White House.

This summer revealed ugly truths about Trump and the tens of thousands who came to town for a Capitol coup.

Trump's plot seared into the public mind more deeply during the Jan. 6 committee hearings in June and July. Witness after witness told of his goading a murderous mob on a day

Congress was captive in the Capitol—hunting to hang Vice President Mike Pence.

Congress met to certify Biden's victory, as the Constitution requires. Within moments of the mob's break-in, crossing police, hundreds were under siege, huddled in the House chamber. Under siege in the "People's House."

Americans have never seen what we have seen in events leading up to the unforgettable summer of '22.

Going into fall, may Biden's luck of the Irish calm our nation's burn—in nature and politics.

Our Towns:
Jan. 6 Justice Done — And Alive Again

Sept. 7, 2022

WASHINGTON — Justice came face-to-face with Thomas Webster, 56, a veteran New York cop who beat a D.C. cop with a Marine flagpole at the Jan. 6, 2021, riot.

I witnessed the courtroom drama. The judge handed down the stiffest sentence yet for a Jan. 6 defendant: 10 years for the first aggressor to break the police line guarding the Capitol.

"I take no pleasure," Judge Amit Mehta spoke from the bench.

"But it was not just one day," Mehta said. "That (darkest) day continues to tear the fabric of this country.

"I still remain shocked every single time I see the 46-second video (of violent rage) ... He was an everyday American. What conditions could have created that?"

Webster addressed Mehta: "The worst part is not jail. It's the shame I have standing here. My kids don't look at me the same way."

The "beautiful family" did not appear by Webster's side as his sentence was meted out.

The Metropolitan police officer Webster knocked to the ground sat in the back row in uniform. Webster turned and declared, "I want to apologize to you, Officer (Noah) Rathbun."

Belated remorse, better than none.

I was inside the Capitol that tragic winter day and saw the siege of our democracy's temple. A heartbreak and an outrage, all in the name of former President Donald Trump.

Will the 45th president ever face a judge? You tell me.

Walking uphill in the Cathedral Heights neighborhood, I passed an English friend's house. I had not seen her since the pandemic. I remembered a small garden party where she served an English elderflower drink. Delightful.

And there she was, walking down to her house.

She invited me in for — was it too much to hope for? — an elderflower cordial to catch up. We said it would be sad when summer cicadas stopped singing.

The Library of Congress puts on the National Book Festival on Labor Day weekend. The crossroads of thousands brings authors, families, readers and C-SPAN, the city chronicler, together in the thousands.

Founded by first lady Laura Bush in 2001, the Festival missed two years of live events, in 2020 and 2021. Brimming to be back in person.

In line for lattes and macchiatos, I was shoulder to shoulder with a woman I worked with once at The Baltimore Sun. Her voice sounded so familiar it was time travel.

She's now at The Washington Post, covering the White House. Her beau works there as a columnist.

"I just tag along," he said, smiling.

As it happened, she was headed to my hometown, Madison, Wisconsin, to speak at the annual Idea festival. That impressed me greatly.

I suggested the Memorial Union Terrace as a happy place to interview university students on the fall battleground races.

Then I found the author table. David Maraniss signed his magnificent new biography of Jim Thorpe, "Path Lit by Lightning."

"I know this one," he said, meaning me.

We share the same hometown. His father Elliott was editor of The Capital Times.

David's bestseller tells of the legendary athlete's life, colored by the American Indian experience of being trampled upon by government policy for two centuries.

A flash of justice, he told listeners, crossed Thorpe's path. He starred on his Carlisle Indian Industrial School football team in the 1912 game against West Point.

"It was the Indians against the Army," Maraniss said.

The Indians won while "the ghosts of history hovered." Dwight Eisenhower, an Army linebacker, liked to say he tackled Thorpe—once.

The Sept. 11 terrorist attacks happened days after the first Festival on the National Mall.

If you think about it, Jan. 6 was even more grave. A foreign plot with 19 guys (15 Saudis) versus a mob of 30,000 Americans waging a war within.

By chance, I ran into more friends from Baltimore at the end of the day. We went out to dinner on the soft summer night. Unbidden.

Our towns are alive again. That felt good. The playwright of "Our Town," Thornton Wilder, was born in Madison.

Cicadas still sing. For now.

Why Trump Talks Nonstop About Witch Hunts

Sept. 28, 2022

No American president ever posed as the victim of a "witch hunt"—save former President Donald Trump. It's his favorite metaphor for all time and place.

We'll be hearing more of that as courts and the House committee on Jan. 6 trace a long trail of crimes under investigation, up to the failed Capitol coup. Justice may bring punishment. Certainly a 2024 campaign is going out the window.

But let's focus on Trump's obsession with "witch hunts." The decadent Mar-a-Lago dweller has no shame in stealing a metaphor that belongs to us—women.

Yet it turns out Trump does have a close connection with witch hunts. His sordid mentor, Roy Cohn, was the chief counsel to Sen. Joseph McCarthy's committee that blacklisted "communists" in Washington, New York and Hollywood during the 1950s.

For those who celebrate history, this is when it rhymes.

You and I know that mostly women suffered as they were accused, tried and hanged as witches in the Old and New Worlds.

Indulged all his miscreant life, Trump has nothing in common with innocent people who looked persecution in the eye.

Maybe you've heard of the medieval ducking pond test: If the woman sank to the bottom, that proved she was innocent of witchcraft. Widows, midwives or herb healers were sometimes suspected of having unnatural powers.

September was the month when the Puritan town of Salem, Massachusetts, put to death the largest number of "witches." Nine died, witnessed by the village. The year was 1692, and here we are still talking about witch hunts and trials, exactly 330 years later.

One Salem man, Giles Corey, was pressed to death with stones on Sept. 19. His wife Martha was hanged. The scenes were ugly as neighbors saw neighbors go to the gallows by the hill. Rebecca Nurse, 71, was condemned, despite an outcry. All told, 20 died in 1692, which left deep wounds in the small colonial village.

All were judged by men cloaked in legal and religious power.

Puritans were harsh on themselves, too. Five years later, a witch trial judge, Samuel Sewall, expressed remorse before a Boston church congregation, stating he "desires to take the blame and shame of it."

Try to imagine Trump taking "the blame and shame" of his actions. That takes courage. He would never do it, for he is always the victim.

The witch hunts were chalked up to "mass hysteria."

If you ask me, what ailed the Puritans is still with us today. It just has a different name: QAnon beliefs spread rapidly among Trump supporters. They showed up in force in the deadly mob attack on the Capitol on Jan. 6, 2021.

QAnon is a bizarre political conspiracy theory that I don't even want to describe in polite company. But it's giving Trump one last gasp of hope for a strong base of support.

The more desperate Trump is, the harder he'll fall into QAnon believers. He's warned of inciting violence again: "the likes of which perhaps we've never seen."

His lackey, Sen. Lindsey Graham, R-S.C., chimed in that street "riots" were ahead if Trump was indicted.

One of the great American playwrights, Arthur Miller spent time in Salem going over the court records of the 1692 tragedies.

The drama he wrote, in the early 1950s, "The Crucible," is a theater classic.

Miller held up the McCarthy era hearings to the light of Salem's zealous pursuit of (so-called) witches. He created characters based on what was known, with their real names. He revealed the alarm started in the Rev. Samuel Parris' house and took flight like lightning.

Telling the Salem story, Miller showed how easy it was to suggest or spread lies, even among god-fearing people.

Miller witnessed it in his own time, with writers called before McCarthy's committee to "name names." Some did, some did not. Those named — in government, journalism, the arts — had their lives ruined.

McCarthy kept pressing until the day he was stopped by an Army lawyer, Joseph Welch: "Have you no sense of decency?"

The answer was no. Nor did dark Cohn have a shred of decency as he egged on McCarthy's evil deeds. He later taught them to young Trump.

The Good, the Bad and the Ugly

Oct. 12, 2022

WASHINGTON — Our town awaits with bated breath as a beautiful autumn falls on the midterm campaigns and the sedition trial of five "Oath Keepers."

And we miss the murdered Rose Garden.

The 2022 election for Congress is a real tug of war — some even say "civil war."

What happens in close races will affect the air we breathe in the capital. If the Democratic Senate stays blue and the House tips Republican red, then divided government will have a whole new toxic meaning.

The battleground would likely be House hearings versus the Biden White House or family. It won't be pretty, especially if bulldog Rep. Jim Jordan, R-Ohio, becomes Judiciary Committee chairman.

Because the country, after all, needs further tearing apart.

The extremist Oath Keepers champion civil war. They're the pro-Donald Trump outfit that marched into the Capitol riot on Jan. 6, 2021, in military "stack" formation. One carried bear spray into the building and threatened Capitol police officers, the indictment charged.

Their founder, Stewart Rhodes, is a former Army paratrooper and Yale Law School graduate. In the weeks before the deadly Capitol riot, Rhodes was in contact with a friend of then-President Trump, Roger Stone, according to the court case.

Court documents show a chilling obsession with keeping the defeated Trump in power, even if relying on violence and bloodshed. The Oath Keepers kept a stash of weapons across the river for a "quick reaction force."

I went to the courthouse to see these characters face justice, a judge and jury. Charged as co-conspirators, the five face long sentences, but the damage they did lingers long after the mob stormed the Capitol.

Jan. 6 was the day the Oath Keepers' dreams of an anti-government coup almost came true. They trained and traveled from all points — like Florida and Texas — to overthrow the congressional ritual to certify Joe Biden as the winner in the 2020 presidential election.

Rhodes, 56, wears an eye patch and cuts a somewhat squat figure for one in the line of fire that day. (I was in the House chamber.)

Rhodes invoked "1776" in his online messages, urging members on as if he were George Washington leading a new American revolution. He built the organization with zeal, influencing swaths of followers.

Interestingly, four of the five on trial are military veterans. One was a Navy intelligence officer; the other three joined the Army.

That raises the question of whether an all-volunteer military is a good idea for democracy. It suggests the military self-selects, attracts and trains some men predisposed to militias once out of the armed services.

(Jessica Watkins, a defendant from Ohio, is a trans woman.)

The Anti-Defamation League tracks extremist groups. The mob of tens of thousands besieging the Capitol was no surprise, the League said. The mob made plans on the internet and had a "wanted" list of lawmakers and Mike Pence, the vice president.

Trump loved the three-hour show of violence, gloating over the crowd size that day. He was no doubt pleased with the highest TV ratings he ever had, as the nation watched the siege in horror.

Meanwhile, back at the Capitol: "You are in danger," my sister said from California.

The House committee on the Jan. 6 attack on democracy holds a final hearing Thursday. More news may be broken, but one thing is sure.

By defying the peaceful transfer of power, Trump sowed seeds of election deniers in the Republican Party. They are on the ballot right now, concentrated in Florida and Texas, but all over America.

That may be his greatest gift to the American people in the end.

His wife Melania Trump sowed seeds in the Rose Garden, by scuttling the original Kennedy vision (Jack and Jackie's.) The sulky Mrs. Trump had blossoms, shrubs and trees pulled up for pavement so her husband could walk over it. This was done shortly before the election he lost.

Under a bright sun, people flocked to the White House fall garden — now under new ownership — near the Oval Office. The Rose Garden looked denuded of crab apple trees and colorful flowers.

It's just one more insult with Trump fingerprints on the scene.

Two Blows in One Night to Democracy

Nov. 2, 2022

How social is social media?

Elon Musk, Twitter's new owner, gives a clear answer to that question. Musk made the platform—a public square—his own boiling cauldron of hate just in time for Halloween.

Double blows to American democracy occurred overnight, within hours of each other. It seems a tragedy of Shakespearean proportions.

Enter the ghoulish Musk. He doesn't need a costume.

Then Paul Pelosi, 82, House Speaker Nancy Pelosi's husband, is almost murdered in his bed in their San Francisco home. He resembles good Duncan, the first to die by blood in Macbeth.

In the first act, a convergence of these events happened in real time.

Musk took an unspeakably ugly lie—which I won't repeat—about the Pelosi crime and retweeted it as a "tiny possibility."

Musk, the world's wealthiest man, makes the robber barons look good.

This lie was "amplified" a thousandfold. If the new boss showed "fair is foul and foul is fair," then waging more war on the Speaker in an hour of grief was open season.

We in the press are cast in the play as truth-tellers. Yet we miss a lot, like the Jan. 6 plot.

Our job is not just to breathlessly report tweets. Journalism words like "misinformation," "accountable" and "baseless" are just jargon, way too weak for the alarming cascade of vile abuse heaped on public figures.

The would-be political assassin demanded, "Where's Nancy?"

The Speaker was in San Francisco shortly beforehand, at a Golden Gate National Recreation Area celebration. She had departed for Washington, thank goodness. Days before, the Speaker visited Croatia, keeping the busiest schedule under the sun.

I cover her, unflappable under fire. But this outrageous attack, hitting home, broke her heart.

It shocked and cracked hearts of all decent people, that the venom Speaker Pelosi gets turned into violence *again*.

The Jan. 6 mob stormed the Capitol and shouted her name in the crypt. All they forgot was pitchforks.

Pro-Trump extremist groups like the Oath Keepers became organized and radicalized on the internet. Oath Keepers marched into the Capitol in military gear to overturn the presidential election by force for the first time. The armed throng scaled the steps and terrace.

The latest attack shattered a sense of safety, even complacency, about the harm social media does to us. Yes, we make new friends who are sorry when our dog dies—but at what cost to our collective soul?

Does our obsession bring out the best or worst in the American character? Dependence on devices and friends, known and unknown, deepened during the pandemic.

I can tell you one thing. The darkness festering in social media is not what First Amendment author James Madison meant by free speech. He considered it enlightening exchanges for the *health* of our body politic—not the present tense "discoarse."

One Louisiana Republican, Rep. Clay Higgins, was particularly pitiless in a tweet (deleted) aimed at the Pelosis. No surprise, Donald Trump Jr. sent a trash tweet that never should have made print or air.

House Republican leader Kevin McCarthy of California lifted a finger to send a text to the Speaker.

Meanwhile, before our eyes, Twitter became a pitched battle, an ethereal Gettysburg.

Major names debated, as Dan Rather put it, should I stay or go? I love what the 91-year-old news sage has to say every day, but I can't stay long.

Saudi Arabia is the second largest shareholder in Twitter. The cruel desert kingdom is a dealbreaker for me. Friends and foes, see you on the other side.

John Dean of Watergate infamy bemoaned losing a thousand followers: "I enjoy comments from my followers, so I find this disquieting."

Yes, that's the real tragedy.

Political sage Norm Ornstein is reluctant to leave the site for other reasons. He found a vast community of friends with whom he could share life's vicissitudes and "fulminate about evil and injustice."

I'll miss Norm most when I go. He's generous with his ocean of knowledge about Congress and circulates "great stuff by others."

Ornstein told his circle (over 229,000) of concerns for democracy in coming days: "But I'll stay. For now."

The offstage villain of the play still breathes free air. For now.

Jamie Stiehm

Voters Verdict: End of The Trump Era

Nov. 16, 2022

The country came to its senses last Tuesday, after a seven-year famine in our politics. The worst in our nature showed up in vulgar, violent and virulent former President Donald Trump.

The hard-fought congressional midterms are a turning point in our civil strife. Election Day delivered a crystal-clear verdict from the American people: democracy matters. (More than gas prices.)

Please, sir, more fair and square democracy and decency.

That's what President Biden brings to the table. We keep hearing how unpopular he is, but "Joe" is a hard guy not to like, with a steady hand on the tiller.

Bonhomie works for me.

The improbable dream of Democrats keeping the Senate chamber blue came true before our eyes. The impossible dream of a Democratic House of Representatives victory hangs in the air.

America has plenty to be thankful for on Thanksgiving Thursday.

The majority of voters told us the Trump Republican party's over now. Most of his hand-picked radical Right candidates lost in a rebuke to the bitter, twice-impeached ex-president.

Now he's the madman in the attic.

Can a seven-year era of good times and feelings begin now? We are not enemies, but friends, as Abraham Lincoln pleaded in an inaugural address.

The so-called "red wave" that fooled pundits was dishonest Republican rumors and polls, disinformation the press bought wholesale. (Not me, ma'am.)

This time, their Big Lie spread *before* Election Day. There was never a red wave, to be clear. Every Democrat knew they had a fighting chance to win their own races. Candidates were energized by the extreme Supreme Court decision to strike down reproductive rights in June.

University students and suburban women were furious at the nerve of Trump's trio of icy young justices. They dared to take life, liberty and health choices away, joining senior members for a bombshell majority opinion.

The "Extreme Supremes" are under scrutiny as part of a working democracy. Chief Justice John Roberts says the 6-3 high court should not care if rulings go against the current of popular opinion.

Roberts could not be more wrong.

Six unelected hard-Right Republicans — six! — should not be the boss of 300 million of us. Social progress is the Court's hallmark in sunny days. The legitimacy of the Roberts court is in trouble.

Voters also rejected the political violence Trump espoused. Everyone but him and the 30,000-strong throng that stormed the Capitol knew how terribly wrong that was. Oath Keepers are standing trial now for sedition, facing 20 years behind bars.

The chilling Jan. 6 trauma took time to get over, especially for those of us stuck in the siege.

Further, what turned minds in election season was the brutal hammer attack on Paul Pelosi at home in the dead of night.

We did not want to be that country.

Trump running for president is a great gift to the Democratic party. Send the man a buttery thank-you note.

Republicans know this as they flee for cover from his coarse brand. But the vast swath of slavish Republicans cutting their red ties to him need to go through a "deTrumpification" process.

Victory is sweet, literally. I bet a box of chocolates on a blue Senate.

Yet at least two deserve a box of schadenfreude.

Californian Kevin McCarthy, the House Republican leader, foolishly bragged about surfing to the speakership before the votes were in. Knives are out for him now. He sent only a text to House Speaker Nancy Pelosi when her husband was nearly murdered. And risible Sarah Palin lost for the Alaska House seat.

Sweet was the vision of a beguiling baby girl on the Senate floor, when they came back to business. Almost one year old, Eva Beth Ossoff was calm at the center of attention.

Her father, Sen. Jon Ossoff, D-Ga., bravely took her to meet Minority Leader Mitch McConnell, R-Ky. The baby pointed here, there and up at the lights, a bipartisan treat.

Often politicians are surrounded by babies; here was a baby surrounded by politicians. A baby is a vote for the future.

Meanwhile, over in the People's House, undaunted Pelosi gave an elegant dinner in Statuary Hall and welcomed new Democratic members with their ideas, energy and optimism, she said.

So there.

Giving Thanks to Madam Speaker

Nov. 23, 2022

WASHINGTON—Journalists don't cry. It's in the code of conduct. Yet tears welled in my eyes in the House press gallery when Speaker Nancy Pelosi gave her farewell speech as Speaker, though she will stay on in Congress.

Reader, the stem-winder at high noon brought down the house. Clad in gleaming white, like a modern suffragette, Pelosi delivered one for the ages. Move over, Daniel Webster.

The Speaker reminded the House that this was the "temple of democracy." That the Capitol is "the most beautiful building in the world." And indeed, our democracy is majestic but "fragile."

Everyone in the chamber knew what Pelosi meant. The contrast between the November day and the Jan. 6, 2021, siege could not have been clearer. The mob that stormed the Capitol on a winter day came rushing down the marble halls, hunting for the Speaker.

Members and press found a way to escape, by a hidden staircase and a tunnel. Howls, gunshots and broken glass were the soundtrack. Late into the night, early in the morning dark, we returned and stayed until the last presidential vote was counted for Joe Biden.

In lockdown, Pelosi had the presence of mind to tell Vice President Mike Pence, sheltered in the Capitol: "Don't tell anyone where you are." Character comes out in crisis.

Senate Democratic Leader Chuck Schumer gave a speech of thanksgiving: "Thank you for teaching us... an honor of a lifetime."

The consensus is, the only woman Speaker in history is the greatest, combining light and heat to keep Democrats together.

For me, it was simple. If an 80-year-old woman can go through that trauma and not skip a beat, I can too. Truthfully, I was not as resilient. The Speaker was a valiant beacon in the rocky post-Jan. 6 days. She refused to crack.

The mob incited by a sitting president would never win over her.

Pelosi is the only politician who confronted former President Donald Trump to his face in public or private. Ripping up a state-of-the-Union speech was stagecraft. Impeaching him twice was her decision.

I covered Pelosi through the dark Trump years and witnessed her squared shoulders on Thursday press conferences through the pandemic. She never missed a day. Politics is performance art, especially in an ordeal, and the show went on. The Speaker always dressed for the part.

Sometimes she was the only one keeping the lights on in the Capitol during COVID-19.

The Speaker decided that the late Justice Ruth Bader Ginsburg, "our beloved" Rep. John Lewis and Rep. Elijah Cummings should lie in state in Statuary Hall or out on the steps, where Abraham Lincoln gave his inaugural addresses. She loved breaking history's ground.

To counter Trump's frigid foreign policy, Pelosi invited world leaders to the Capitol for a warm welcome. The head of NATO gave a joint address to Congress, as did the Greek prime minister. The Jordanian king came to the Speaker's balcony.

Then Pelosi went to Ukraine when war broke out. Onto Taiwan to defy China's hold on it. Looking back, I should have known her 20 years as the House Democratic leader was building to a grand finale.

Pelosi chose her moment well, after a two-year partnership with President Biden, like a ray of spring light in the chamber. The Build Back Better infrastructure bill and the Inflation Reduction Act were leaps forward, the latter for climate change.

I loved that she invited tennis great Billie Jean King to celebrate Title IX. She told me it was "heartbreaking" to cancel woman suffrage 1920 celebrations in 2020.

At 6, young Nancy saw her father ("a proud New Dealer") sworn in as a congressman from Baltimore. It was the first time she saw the Capitol.

Over her 35 years in Congress, she noted, a dozen Democratic women became more than 90. The chamber swelled with applause.

Pelosi spoke of her "dear husband Paul," injured in their home, and thanked the myriad well-wishers for his recovery.

The nation's story is, she declared, "Light and love, of patriotism and progress... to make the dreams of today the reality of tomorrow."

Pelosi was then engulfed by cheers, tears and hugs. "She was spent," said a veteran prize-winning photographer.

So was I.

A Dearth — Or Death — Of Charm in the Capitol

Nov. 30, 2022

I wished the Oklahoma Republican senator well in retirement and reminded him of a trip we took years ago when he was a freshman senator, and I was a rookie reporter.

The craggy conservative, James Inhofe, beamed: "You made my day." He made me believe it was so.

It may not sound like much. But such a moment is scarcer all the time. The death of charm has come to the Capitol.

I remember days when senators exchanged smiles, stories, repartee and jests with each other and the press. Massachusetts Sen. Edward Kennedy's booming laugh could be heard by the statues. Sen. Bob Dole's dry wit crackled like Kansas wheat in high summer.

Senators reached "across the aisle" to produce bipartisan legislation from time to time. They seemed to enjoy each other's company. Sen. Robert C. Byrd was the rules enforcer, but also the voice of history, giving learned talks on the Roman Senate.

Once opposing Senate leaders, Tom Daschle and Trent Lott co-authored a book after they left the Senate.

By contrast, House Republican leader Kevin McCarthy, Calif., who resembles a callow fraternity man, barely spits out "Pelosi," about House Speaker Nancy Pelosi, D-Calif.

The death of charm is not a trivial loss in a field where both sides benefit from working together. Proverbial Senate "giants" flourish in warmer climates.

Fifty Senate Democrats could not get one Republican vote for the greatest investment in climate change ever, nor for the Build Back Better infrastructure bill. (Vice President Kamala Harris broke the ties.)

Politicians were once liked for their hearty handshakes, bonhomie and knowing your name. Sen. John McCain, R-Ariz., was exhibit A in this repertoire.

I'll never forget lunch with the Arizona senator and a press aide in the Senate dining room. Tapping the table, McCain demonstrated the Morse code used to contact other prisoners of war in the Hanoi Hilton.

Now the elegant Senate dining room is often empty.

Come January you'll see what I "mean," as Reps. Jim Jordan of Ohio and Marjorie Taylor Greene of Georgia start their charmless offensive against Hunter Biden, Dr. Anthony Fauci and other victims.

House Republicans, with a few exceptions, swim in former President Donald Trump's school of haters. Check out Clay Higgins, R-La., if you dare.

Freshman Rep. Lauren Boebert, R-Colo., takes the cake. On Jan. 6, 2021, her third day on the job, she spoke on the floor and all but threatened, "Madam Speaker (Pelosi), I have constituents outside this building right now."

Among the younger Senate Republicans, without a scintilla of charm for the other side, an Ivy League superiority adds to their surly arrogance.

I'm talking to you, Ted Cruz of Texas and Josh Hawley of Missouri. Cruz, a Princeton man, went on to Harvard Law School. Hawley was educated at Yale Law School.

They are inheritors of Trump's earthy dirt.

We can't be surprised at Trump's new outrage, hosting Nick Fuentes, a white nationalist and Holocaust denier, and the rapper Ye, also a purveyor of hate talk aimed at Jewish people.

Shocked, but not surprised.

Since Trump entered the political stage in 2015 as a presidential candidate who personally cut down each opponent, nothing has been the same since.

The nasty tone Trump displayed as a contender against Hillary Clinton, the Democratic nominee, was just a foretaste.

Trump's inaugural address—spoken with a scowl—warned of "American carnage." Tarnishing that sacred ritual (sounding like a gangster) was the signal to poison the well for his myriad followers in Congress.

Trump's racism and misogyny never rested as president. After he lost reelection, American carnage swarmed the Capitol in the armed mob he incited.

We've reached an inflection point where some Republicans court defying their party leadership: glowering Rand Paul, Rick Scott and veteran Lindsey Graham fit that bill.

Friends and foes agree, Pelosi and President Joe Biden (a creature of Congress) have some old-school charm. Sen. Mitch McConnell knows how to act as a Southern gentleman. They are all in their 80s.

The Senate Republican most capable of charm toward all 99 colleagues is Mitt Romney, 75, of Utah. Inhofe is a vigorous 88.

Note from the press gallery: don't let charm go out with the old.

Washington Wakes up for the Holidays

Dec. 7, 2022

WASHINGTON — It's beginning to look a lot like...Washington. After years of trauma, the capital feels back to itself for Christmas.

The holiday ball for Congress just happened at the White House. The storied Willard Hotel, where Abraham Lincoln stayed days before he was inaugurated, revived the tradition of Christmas carols in the evening.

In Union Station, a magnificent tree, a gift from Norway, stands high. The Capitol tree, thanks to North Carolina, was lighted early this month.

These customs and rituals comfort and cheer a city that was under siege. They give ballast to putting the Jan. 6 armed attack on the Capitol and the pandemic behind us.

Then there was the formal state dinner for the French president, Emmanuel Macron, followed by the Kennedy Center Honors in the red velvet opera house. George Clooney and U2 were among the honorees, giving our town a dusting of glamor.

But it was the sight of Paul Pelosi, the injured husband of House Speaker Nancy Pelosi, that brought down the house. He suffered head wounds from a night intruder in their San Francisco home.

The message he sent, with no words: political violence won't win.

Paul Pelosi represented a victory for those walking wounded — and shut down by COVID-19 — not long ago.

By contrast, Donald and Melania Trump snubbed and skipped the black-tie Kennedy Center event during his White House years. It's a celebration of art and music that helps to heal hard feelings and spread good will on a winter night.

A jagged shard of memory: Melania Trump chose blood-red trees for holiday decor one year, as if to foreshadow the deadly mob attack on the Capitol.

Hard feelings were what Trump's reign was all about.

Yet his latest rage, calling to "terminate" the Constitution didn't rock the boat much. Some Republican senators actually criticized his tirade.

Across America, Trump's tantrums are becoming normalized as the madman or ogre in the attic. His power is on the wane. In addition, the Trump company was just found guilty of tax fraud.

Trump is not a leader of any party anymore, as shown by the defeat of his handpicked Senate candidate, football player Herschel Walker, in Georgia Tuesday.

Under the alabaster, Congress looks like its old self as it rushes to meet a looming deadline for finishing work. While hectic, the rumble feels familiar.

Scars on its spirit, visible last year, are submerged under the last-minute scramble of the 117th Congress.

Thank goodness.

The House is scheduled to vote on a marriage equality act that the Senate already approved, for same-sex and interracial couples.

A cinematic sideshow: Arizona Democrat and co-sponsor Sen. Kyrsten Sinema, dressed in a turquoise sequin skirt, sat next to poker-faced Republican leader Mitch McConnell during the vote.

The landmark bill, a shield for most of those unions, is certain to be signed by President Joe Biden.

Other pressing items are authorizing the national defense act (the massive Pentagon bill), raising the federal debt limit and keeping the government itself open.

The House and Senate may work nights and days until Christmas. That won't hurt them. They'd like to end this session of Congress on a decisive high note, since it began on Jan. 6, 2021, when a fury of rioters made members of Congress run for their lives.

That means firmly putting that day in the past, in reports

and remembrance.

The House committee probing the Jan. 6 attack will release a detailed report for the official record this month.

House Speaker Nancy Pelosi, D-Calif., hosted a gold medal ceremony (Tuesday) in the Rotunda for Capitol and Metropolitan police officers who defended democracy that day.

The city police chief, Robert J. Contee, noted scores of his 800 officers bear scars from the onslaught.

In the face of the mob's sharp objects, bear spray, screams and smoke, Contee told the assembly, "You did not give up or give in."

McConnell and Pelosi profusely thanked the sea of blue uniformed officers in the airy space: "Thank you for saving the country," McConnell said.

Harry Dunn, a Black Capitol Police officer, wept at midnight in the Rotunda after the mob's relentless storm of racism. Tuesday noon, he looked strong and smiling.

Merry Christmas.

The Mob Came for Me, Thee and Democracy: A Vindication

Dec. 21, 2022

Light sweet justice cascaded over me when the Jan. 6 House committee found former President Donald J. Trump the "central cause" and instigator of the deadly mob attack on the Capitol.

This was personal for me and hundreds trapped inside the stone wall siege. Suddenly, we saw a surreal gun standoff in the House chamber and fog in the hallowed Rotunda.

Could this be happening here?

Breaking news of the former president's four criminal referrals ran so deep that I wanted to stand and sing a glorious hallelujah chorus. The most serious is inciting the insurrection.

The resounding message from the House committee rings clear and true across the land. Political violence against the peaceful transfer of power is the worst high crime you can commit in a democracy.

Unforgettable and unforgivable.

To wit, the rule of law prevailed over a demagogue who tried with all his might to undo a free and fair election. Trump "summoned" the armed mob to storm Congress as it gathered to certify President Joe Biden's 2020 victory, as committee chairman Rep. Bennie Thompson, a Mississippi Democrat, stated. They came in full force.

We all saw the picture show. Now we know the script, thanks to a thousand witness interviews the committee conducted over 18 months.

But I didn't even let myself hope for or expect four referrals to the Justice Department for criminal prosecution. One would have been fine and fitting. But four shows the legislative branch exercised the full reach of its constitutional powers.

Four criminal referrals means American democracy lives

to fight another day. One year ends and another begins on a note of hope.

I might add that trauma is often the last thing to leave a body. The sound of the murderous mob breaking glass and howling down the marble halls haunted my dreams for months. Members of Congress say the same.

Some senators wept as they rushed off the floor, single file, down an old staircase. Some House members took off their jackets to rumble.

The ripples of the committee's report will have wide implications for the Republican party.

There's reason to believe the committee investigation paints such a gruesome picture of Trump that he'll never see the light of political day again. He watched the rampage of the Capitol for three hours with relish. Never had his ratings soared so high.

The most serious charge, inciting an insurrection, all but ends Trump's nasty, brutish and short political career. He has haunted and taunted us long enough. The ball is in the Justice Department's court, whether to pursue criminal prosecutions.

Whatever happens, the People's House has spoken.

The price Trump will pay in personal humiliation will be high when his loyal Republican base rebuffs him as the worst Scrooge-like loser ever to come along in American presidential politics.

Just in time for Christmas, this gift from the House: the word that the government is not Trump's personal property. One man cannot besmirch the parchment of our founders.

Globally, the world was watching closely to see if the "last best hope of earth" had lost or won a war within.

Indelible memories of that day are already healing. It's amazing what a truthful reckoning can do for the doer and his myriad victims.

Given the gravity of sedition, how lucky was the nation to witness the most flawless teamwork ever on a major congressional committee.

That Jan. 6 select panel is part of outgoing House Speaker Nancy Pelosi's lasting legacy. She hand-picked each member.

I keep going back to Trump's black leather gloves that day, as if to hide his fingerprints on the crime scene. He spoke like a true don while Congress was captive inside the Capitol.

Tens of thousands, whipped into a fury, headed toward the alabaster dome a mile away. The mob climbed terrace walls, broke police lines, rushed the marble steps.

The inviting terrace was designed by Frederick Law Olmsted, the landscape architect of Central Park, meant to connect the Capitol with "we the people." What a tragic turn of the screw.

The British redcoats, who burned the Capitol in 1814, had a fair reason: we were two nations at war.

Note to all: not to take precious democracy for granted.

The House Showed the Senate the Way, Time After Time

Dec. 28, 2022

The People's House to Senate: hello, we are what American democracy — and demographics — look like. The upper Capitol chamber is more country, while the House is more city.

The Senate, the "world's greatest deliberative body," is growing old — literally. It does not deserve all the credit when the House does all the work.

Diverse House Democrats turned in a bravura performance after the Jan. 6, 2021, Capitol riot smoke cleared. The two-year session ends Monday, when the new 118th Congress comes in.

In this tragic yet fruitful session of Congress, House lawmakers starkly showed senators how it's done for the greater good.

They are the little engine that could, nudging the big 50-50 Senate train stuck on the tracks.

The Senate rule requiring 60 votes to overcome the brakes (a filibuster) is a huge impediment to the divided body moving forward on most fronts.

Voting rights and extending the equal rights amendment for women, for example, were bills the House passed with robust Democratic majority support.

Despite an eloquent plea from Sen. Raphael Warnock, D-Ga., the Senate killed a path for one — with a little help from Kyrsten Sinema, I-Ariz. The Senate didn't vote on the other.

The Democratic House voted to codify reproductive rights when the Supreme Court lashed out at the Roe v. Wade constitutional case. (The Republican 6-3 majority is no friend to the people.)

The rights bill passed the House with flying colors, but failed in the Senate, with 49 votes.

Sen. Joe Manchin, a West Virginia Democrat, broke with his party. Yet he criticized the high Court for striking down "the law of the land."

The Senate is often skewed and twisted like that.

It would help to get rid of the 60-vote rule for most legislation. Ironically, the sleepy Senate could do this with 51 votes.

In the woke House, everyone knows where everyone stands. It's like homeroom, majority rules.

Right-wing Republicans will take over the House majority with more plans to tear it down than build it up. They are in disarray and can't reach consensus on the next Speaker. Good luck, guys.

House Speaker Nancy Pelosi, D-Calif., directed her disciplined caucus to making major marks on social progress.

The Respect for Marriage (equality) bill became law this month, a sweet swan song for the Speaker, stepping down as the House Democratic leader. Hakeem Jeffries of Brooklyn will succeed her.

Democratic House members, galvanized by the Jan. 6 mob storming the Capitol as the session started, did not flinch in the face of outgoing President Donald Trump's violent plot to undo the 2020 election.

Quite the opposite. The legislative branch used its co-equal power to pursue the first attempted coup in American history.

A vast swath remembered the sounds: broken glass, gunfire and howls ricocheting in the marble halls.

The House, not the Senate, conducted a brilliant investigation of the armed mob attack. Interviewing a thousand witnesses, the select committee report concluded the cause came down to "one man": Trump.

The Senate had defeated naming an independent Jan. 6 commission, so Pelosi decided the House would go it alone.

The House impeached Trump twice. The Senate failed to convict him twice—on grave offenses.

The first charge was trying to bribe a foreign leader, Ukraine's Volodymyr Zelenskyy, for political gain. Later, Trump was impeached by the House for inciting the deadly mob attack on the Capitol.

Just seven Republican senators joined all 50 Democrats in voting to convict the former president. Two-thirds (67 members) of the Senate are needed to turn the president out of office.

The House's greatest unsung act was to finally approve making lynching a federal hate crime. It took years and a former Black Panther, Democratic Rep. Bobby Rush of Chicago, to make it happen.

Rush named the act for Emmett Till, the Chicago youth murdered in Mississippi while visiting family down South. His 1955 lynching was a catalyst for the civil rights movement.

Rush, who's retiring at 76, told me Till relatives came to the House chamber to witness the vote. The Senate then passed the anti-lynching legislation by voice vote. President Joe Biden signed it into law in the spring. Emmett Till and his mother, Mamie Till-Mobley, were awarded the Congressional Gold Medal in the closing days of Congress.

The House saved the soul of America.

Full House Theater: An American Tragedy

Jan. 11, 2023

WASHINGTON — A full House for four days and four nights felt like 40 in the political wilderness.

Pumping his fist like a frat bro, California Republican Rep. Kevin McCarthy eked out a victory for House speaker. Even then, the man from Bakersfield showed no gravitas.

Look it up, Kevin.

Brooklyn's Rep. Hakeem Jeffries, the new Democratic leader, showed steady poise and smarts straight out of "Hamilton."

Witnessing the marathon roll votes from the press gallery, I tried *not* to remember the mob Donald Trump sent to the Capitol on Jan. 6, 2021.

I sat frozen in the same spot then. Gunfire, grunts and broken glass still echo, two years on.

The raucous House denied McCarthy, 57, the 218 votes needed in 14 roll call votes.

In deep time, we were back on the brink of civil war. That was the last time a speaker vote lasted longer than McCarthy's.

The strange thing happening was not only a House divided, but a war waged within Republican ranks.

The Right versus the hard Right was not a pretty picture. (No moderates to soften the mix.)

By the end of the midnight chamber drama, McCarthy gave the House away to 20 extremists.

Meaning, he bargained away so much power that he'll have little left. Not that he cares.

The title's the thing.

All McCarthy wanted was to wrest the gavel from Democrats. No principles or rules were too sacred to sacrifice.

After all, the leader first blamed Trump for the deadly Capitol riot, then visited him in Mar-a-Lago.

Among the most reckless parts of McCarthy's "deal" endangers the House ethics committee and the debt ceiling, which guarantees the full faith and credit of the United States.

Experts say government shutdowns are in our future — and jams in the way Congress conducts business and funds social programs.

We'll also have a slew of sham "investigations" by the hater Rep. Jim Jordan, R-Ohio. Just wait.

America will soon see the new Republican majority, especially the "Freedom Caucus," did not go to Washington as believers in good governing.

They came to paralyze democracy, and they did it on the first day.

Texan Rep. Chip Roy, once chief of staff to Sen. Ted Cruz, was one leader of the Republican mutiny.

Pugnacious Rep. Scott Perry, R-Pa., was another. He dared to compare Frederick Douglass to their cause. Rep. Kweisi Mfume, D-Md., a former president of the NAACP, was not amused.

An aggressive pair of Arizona Republicans, Reps. Andy Biggs and Paul Gosar, also voted against McCarthy.

Across the aisle, Speaker emerita Nancy Pelosi, D-Calif., sat in back benches, bemused at the chaos McCarthy wrought.

If this was political theater, Republicans could not get their act together.

Lauren Boebert, R-Colo., a sophomore member of Congress, was a vocal holdout against McCarthy, declaring on the floor that he should quit the race.

The Trump loyalist spoke as the mob advanced two years ago: "Madam Speaker, I have constituents outside this building right now."

Speak, memory.

Between votes, McCarthy told reporters, "It's not how you start, it's how you finish," as if it was biblical wisdom.

Within the anti-McCarthy faction, Rep. Matt Gaetz of Florida, seen as a lightweight troublemaker, rose and made the most cutting comment on his character.

Gaetz bluntly stated that McCarthy had "sold shares of himself" to become speaker. The irony of him voicing a Democratic lament was lost.

After a near-brawl, Gaetz voted "present" to give McCarthy the prize he craved.

Democrats stayed solid in a Greek chorus of 212. A Marylander, Rep. David Trone, had surgery one morning and returned in the afternoon.

The Democratic caucus bonded in a baptism by fire, under new management.

Jeffries and his leadership team, Reps. Katherine Clark, Mass., and Pete Aguilar, Calif., proved worthy of the hour.

Once the dirty deal was done, Jeffries, 52, gave a speech that landed like Demosthenes, the Athenian orator. He struck a sore nerve in praising "the peaceful transfer of power."

Violence may break out again, since McCarthy removed the metal detectors for members entering the floor, the Pelosi rule.

Then an epiphany: few Republicans in this House ever denounced Trump. Most challenged the 2020 election results.

Methinks this time, the mob wore a sea of red ties and dark suits.

The Three Women of San Francisco

Jan. 18, 2023

WASHINGTON — So, what city gave America the only woman House speaker, the most senior senator and the first woman vice president?

San Francisco, of course, that fair city.

But here in Washington, nobody knows this.

Few give props to San Francisco for making — or breaking — American history. But a trifecta of Democratic women in high places is no coincidence.

What's in the water there (so to speak?) No other city comes close.

As a journalist who's seen them in action and once lived in the late great columnist Herb Caen's "City," let me offer some thoughts on Rep. Nancy Pelosi, Sen. Dianne Feinstein and Vice President Kamala Harris. Two are truly great.

Pelosi held the speakership for eight of the last 14 years. At 82, she's speaker emerita, clearing the way for the next generation to take the House Democratic torch.

The new leader, Rep. Hakeem Jeffries of New York, praised her as "the greatest Speaker of all time." Congressional expert Norm Ornstein agrees.

You probably know her heroics on Jan. 6, 2021, the day an armed mob stormed the Capitol, some howling and hunting for her by name.

Pelosi showed grace under pressure, calling governors and the Pentagon to send the National Guard (which showed up after the damage was done.)

I witnessed the siege and will never forget that Pelosi and Vice President Mike Pence insisted Congress finish the job of counting electoral votes.

At 4 a.m. by the Capitol's Ohio Clock, democracy won the day.

During the forlorn pandemic, Pelosi kept the lights on in

the Capitol. She didn't miss a day, giving her Thursday press conferences in person, striding in with a bright mask.

During the Donald Trump years, Pelosi was the only lawmaker to stand up to him to his face. Oh, how he hated her for initiating two impeachments and the Jan. 6 committee.

The violence Trump incited could have been much worse, but it claimed 150 police casualties.

What you may not know is that Pelosi was packed to go to Afghanistan, when Trump canceled the military plane.

Conducting diplomacy, Pelosi invited foreign leaders to Washington, such as the NATO secretary general and the Greek prime minister.

Pelosi also visited Ukraine last year. As her last act, she had President Volodymyr Zelenskyy deliver a speech, a riveting hour that united the chambers and parties.

I liked lighter moments, too. The St. Patrick's Day luncheon with the Irish leader was a tradition.

Sen. Dianne Feinstein is such a fixture in San Francisco politics, from when she was mayor, that she's taken for granted as she approaches age 90. Tall and regal, her speaking manner is more formal than Pelosi's warmth.

Feinstein rushed to dying Supervisor Harvey Milk and Mayor George Moscone when they were assassinated in City Hall in 1978.

That tragedy put her on the path to the Senate in 1992. That was known as the "Year of the Woman" because women were aghast at how an all-male Senate panel handled the Supreme Court confirmation hearings for one Clarence Thomas.

(I remember listening by radio from my soccer team game in Golden Gate Park, our river of anger rising.).

As a freshman senator, Feinstein authored a 10-year ban on assault weapons that became law. That established her as a force to respect in the clubby Senate.

Serving on the Intelligence committee, Feinstein went public with a CIA report on torture practices during the Iraq

War.

That was moral courage.

Yet Feinstein is fading. The job is punishing. She could be president pro tem, fourth in line to the presidency, but chose to decline.

Feinstein should retire with the dignity her career deserves, in the 2024 election cycle.

Vice president Kamala Harris, 58, is still earning her spurs. Washington is watching, but she hasn't won people over.

In a field for extroverts, Harris seems cool, and needs a success of her own. She requested voting rights, which came up short in the Senate.

Washington is a masculine city, if there ever was one, with marble memorials to presidents and generals.

San Francisco's scenic hills, bridges, fog, bay and skyscape colors created a city of free spirits and pioneers.

Pioneers like these three women.

Brash Young Governor Trumps Trump

March 22, 2023

The ace Gov. Rick DeSantis brings to the 2024 Republican table is simple: he won't be indicted any day now.

An angry young man, 44, next to angry old Donald Trump, DeSantis is no treat. He's learned his lessons well about hard Right, mean-spirited politics—from Trump himself.

The word "woke" is his front line of attack, tampering with original Black slang. It means an aware state of knowing the social cards stacked against you.

Armed with a Harvard Law degree, DeSantis is an even more dangerous man.

Democrats should not let down their game if the sullen Florida sourpuss overtakes Trump as the Republican frontrunner for president.

As well he might.

Trump looks his age, 76. Despite his bitter bluster, he knows it's deeply humiliating to get arrested on a criminal charge, whether on Tuesday or not.

As a president brimming with hate, dealing in insults, boasts and lies, his animal sense may know the jig is up. It's a first for a former president.

Yet he has the gall to run again, not to go gentle into that garish night, Mar-a-Lago.

Let it not be forgot Trump lost the popular vote to Hillary Clinton and Joe Biden—by 7 million votes in 2020. The Jan. 6 Trump mob storming the Capitol made his stock plunge with all but the most rabid followers.

Pity the Republican party if they back a nominee with the law catching up with him in New York, Georgia and with Justice special counsel for Trump probes, Jack Smith. A porn actress payoff may be just the start of Trump's tangled web of woes.

Actually, don't pity the party. There are only a few good

men left. House Speaker Kevin McCarthy, a super-shallow California Republican, is not of them.

Even Trump's most avid devotees are quietly losing faith. A thousand were arrested for the Capitol breach and its violent crimes. Extremist groups, military veterans, former cops and everyday Americans are now sentenced to prison, one by one.

The message is unmistakable: A personal price is paid for joining a murderous mob against the government.

Another proud first in American history.

I've seen some defendants weep as they face the judge and beg for mercy, such as the Confederate flag carrier and the bare-chested man with helmet and horns.

Onto DeSantis. If he's an adept candidate with a bit of chemistry, he could turn MAGA sound and fury into a spring wind. Still undeclared, he can present as a safer bet.

First, the Southern governor could brag about his inhumanity, as a Navy lawyer on Guantanamo. He looked up the book on how to force-feed detainees, suspects on hunger strikes. Keep in mind these were men jailed for long years, never brought to a court trial.

(President Barack Obama broke his pledge to close the island jail, a known burn pit for human rights.)

Second, DeSantis singling out gay and transgender young people proves he's good at picking on the most vulnerable among us. That's his way of the world, a strategic skill in the post-Trump party he clearly hopes to lead.

Meanwhile, public school teachers and librarians in Florida are under a culture siege from a new state law DeSantis has pushed.

All books available to schoolchildren must be vetted and approved. Florida's rows of empty bookshelves are a sad sight for young minds.

That signals fear and dread spreading among people who dedicate their lives to kids learning. Policing minds is contagious.

Also, DeSantis shows a Trumpian lust for revenge. When Disney dared to differ with him on gender and gay issues, down came its own self-governing district. DeSantis will now control the board and government relations of the tourist giant, Disney World.

Like Trump's Supreme Extreme Court, DeSantis marches in goose step against constitutional rights for women *and girls*. Beyond six weeks, he concurs, is too late to legally end a pregnancy.

Word is, DeSantis is brighter than Trump, so he's capable of doing more harm, pressing levers of law and power against the American people.

Stay woke to DeSantis, my friends. As long as he stays at the table, he may play a trump card.

The Day That Justice Comes for Trump, One Senator Never Surrenders

April 5, 2023

WASHINGTON — Mark the moment in time, the day the jam of justice broke for former President Donald Trump at last in court, where he was arraigned for criminal charges.

Who says April is the cruelest month?

That word "criminal" — cherish it, while others rage and weep, like South Carolina senator Lindsey Graham, a Republican who gleefully participated in President Bill Clinton's persecution over a perfectly legal affair that involved no hush money or constitutional offense.

For Graham, hypocrisy is nothing new. Some Republican senators are secretly pleased — hello, Mitt Romney and Mitch McConnell — but Graham is making the loudest noise over Trump's indictment. The reason why is worth knowing.

Trump, the nefarious New Yorker who lied, cheated and stole his way to the presidency, stoking flames of anger against Blacks and women, is a desperate man.

It shows up in his social media messages: he spelled "indicted" as "indicated." Not that he was ever a master of the English language.

Trump knows, with peasant cunning, this is the end of the glory road for him. He knows that other cases are coming for him. The Justice Department and the state of Georgia are not far behind.

Inciting an armed mob against the government, refusing to surrender top-secret files and trying to pressure state officials to change the outcome in a presidential election is not small fry.

Then there's possible tax fraud and a civil rape trial. When it rains, it pours, Donald, on the most vulgar confidence man in the American pantheon of politics. No tears, no mercy, no pardon.

Everyone, enjoy this day. It belongs to the rule of law. Ironically, Trump seems to realize the gravity of his jeopardy more than some pundits and friends, who fret that Alvin Bragg, the Manhattan district attorney, has brought the weakest case against Trump to the light of day.

What this historic indictment may do is intensify Trump's already-ardent support from one faction of the electorate. But Trump is not going to win any new voters this way. And he lost the 2020 election by a margin of 7 million votes. He lost the popular vote in 2016.

Graham, in a defiant Fox News interview, declared, "This is going to destroy America. We're going to fight back at the ballot box... How does this end? Trump wins in court and he wins the (2024) election."

Dream on, Lindsey. Consider the source: South Carolina consistently produces the bad apples of American politics. Segregationist Strom Thurmond and John Calhoun were senators from the Palmetto State.

Calhoun defended antebellum slavery forcefully and developed the concepts of secession, states' rights and nullification, the legal justifications for the Civil War, which he did not live to see.

The late Sen. Ernest Hollings, D-S.C., rowed against the tide, one of the more delightful senators to hear on the floor.

When I began covering Capitol Hill, the seething hatred for President Clinton among House Speaker Newt Gingrich's Republican ranks was striking. It was personal, reader. They were just jealous.

Mean-spirited as they come, the younger Graham relished his place on the House Judiciary Committee when impeachment proceedings were launched. Chairman Henry Hyde and his dozen unearthed tons of salacious details about Clinton's brief consensual relationship with a woman of age.

The cudgel beat on and crossed to the more sensible Senate, which acquitted Clinton. The press mass hysteria was hard to watch. While the affair was wrong, it was private, and certainly not criminal. No questions should be asked about that under oath in a star chamber.

Brett Kavanaugh, now a Supreme Court Justice, served as Independent Counsel Kenneth Starr's enforcer and all but abducted Lewinsky. He questioned, threatened and held the young woman (with no lawyer.)

So, when Kavanaugh, Trump's nominee, came under fire for possible sexual assault, the partisan Graham shouted that others were "trying to destroy this guy's life." He used the word "crap," as he's wont to do. "This is the most despicable thing I have seen in my time in politics."

Graham's loyalty to Trump is like his kinship with the late strong-minded Sen. John McCain, R-Ariz. He played McCain's Sancho Panza on the Hill. When McCain died, Trump filled that void in his heart.

Gathering Storm Shows House Republicans Have No Limits

May 10, 2023

WASHINGTON — Anxiety mounted here as President Joe Biden met with four congressional leaders Tuesday to discuss the financial crisis coming home to hit Americans. No resolution is in sight.

The global economy is also at stake, facing an emergency if the national debt limit isn't raised by Congress for the president's signing. Much depends on the anchor of the Treasury's "full faith and credit."

It's so simple. All Congress must do is vote to increase the debt ceiling for money (and tax cuts) already spent. Like always. It happens all the time, for presidents of each party, for over 100 years.

That's fair play; Democrats cooperated with former President Donald Trump. But belligerent Republicans won't with Biden. A "clean" bill, with no conditions, is the time-honored custom.

Raising the Treasury debt ceiling should not even be up for discussion.

Failure to do so is a recipe for recession and a stock market in free fall.

However, a rowdy House Republican crowd whose motto could be "Biden delenda" cares little for you and me. Their treacherous threat to block raising the debt limit adds up to more election denial.

One Lauren Boebert, a Colorado Republican, chillingly shouted on Jan. 6, 2021, "Madam Speaker, I have constituents outside this building right now."

Three of the four men meeting in the Oval could chart a way out of the gathering storm. That includes Senate Republican Leader Mitch McConnell of Kentucky, the old war horse who has seen it all come and go.

But House Speaker Kevin McCarthy, R-Calif., captive to the Republican hard Right, is not searching for solutions. The grandstanding new speaker is scaring the wits out of those who fear he'd let the Treasury default for the first time in history.

Maybe rash McCarthy really would; maybe he's not bluffing.

What's sure is McCarthy's fealty to (about 50) members who are openly pro-Trump and anti-government. He barely won the Speakership. The "Freedom Caucus" put him over the top, wringing concessions like this grave moment of danger.

And so, McCarthy crafted a bill with their drastic demands—slashing climate, veterans, students and other social programs—which passed with indicted freshman George Santos, R-N.Y., casting the deciding vote.

McCarthy is passing it off as a legitimate bill to Biden in exchange for the House Republican majority raising the debt ceiling.

News: When a president is elected by the people, you can't undermine all he stands for, everything he passed into law with harsh revenge measures that have no chance in the upper chamber.

The British would say, it's just not "done" to seize the common good to blackmail Biden.

Ancient Rome's last war against Carthage, its main maritime rival, comes to mind. Rome became ruthless.

First, Carthage had to hand over 300 children. Then, trumpets sounded as its army surrendered all weapons to Roman envoys. Then the envoys broke the really bad news— the city must be destroyed: "Carthago delenda est."

Rome really meant it.

Scipio, the Roman general, lay siege to Carthage. The Romans razed and burnt the shimmering city by the sea and sold its remaining population into slavery. Scipio wept at the sight.

Did someone say "siege"? I remember a siege of our own Capitol, all too well. The marble temple was built with Rome in mind. It took more than a thousand police officers to defend it.

Trump sent that armed mob to overthrow democracy. Never forget it. McCarthy and his allies are in league with him.

The historian Richard Miles observed that Carthage's fall led to Rome's "bitter discord" at home and civil war.

Let's learn from the past for a change.

Yet the public does not know the urgency of the peril.

Democrats are failing to get the message out that the economy could crater as early as June 1 — if the Treasury can't pay its bills.

The nation would plunge into unknown straits, with job losses, missed Social Security payments, higher interest rates and other severe consequences. Plus the global fall from grace.

Biden should wisely refuse to choose between two catastrophic choices. His only course is the clean path to raising the debt ceiling, even if he does it alone, without Congress.

The Best of the Worst: Republicans for President

June 14, 2023

As Donald Trump grimly faces the first federal criminal indictment ever handed down to a president, let's consider his competition in the Republican primary.

My father challenged me to pick "the best of the worst" in the wide field of Republican men—and a woman, former Gov. Nikki Haley—contesting Trump in the 2024 race.

I'll cover the most viable, visible candidates. Many were acolytes and allies of Trump.

Quick, who is that North Dakota governor again? Doug Burgum outlawed reproductive rights for women and girls even if they are victims of rape and incest (after six weeks of pregnancy.) In Hollywood script talk, that's a room-emptier.

So, no go for forced births. Sorry, gov.

And that brash biotech businessman Vivek Ramaswamy, who knows nothing about political history? He vows to pardon Trump if elected. That's it. He's out.

Then there's the rough-hewn New Jerseyan, a former governor who claims to see the light about Trump at last. Chris Christie is his name. Have you ever seen him dance at a Bruce Springsteen concert? Not very... presidential. But that's the least of it.

Untrustworthy Christie was all in for Trump until he wasn't, like last week. He helped Trump prepare for his 2020 campaign debates with Joe Biden. He must be a terrible judge of character if he's only now denouncing his political paragon for the 37-count federal indictment, including acts of espionage and conspiracy.

Most of these people seem unpleasant, a far cry from the days when politicians had a ready smile, handshake and a good word for folks.

Who wants to have a beer with sour Florida Gov. Ron

DeSantis? So far, his nastiness is unsurpassed, except for Trump. He's declared war on a major employer and tourist attraction in his state, Disney World, the LGBTQ community, library freedom and reproductive rights for women and girls.

Very nice, as if DeSantis learned his manners on Guantanamo, where he worked as a naval lawyer overseeing the treatment of detainees in the military island jail. So, no way.

South Carolina's Tim Scott, the one Black Republican in the Senate, has an affable demeanor. Yet he wanders a bit aimlessly and has little to show and say for his 10 years, other than party-line votes. He's out.

Haley, also of South Carolina, is the only woman in the field. She served in the Trump administration as ambassador to the United Nations and distinguished herself in the international body with her sharp tongue.

That's a key trait, which she showed again by loudly claiming that a vote for President Biden was a vote for President Kamala Harris, almost like a death wish for the 80-year-old president.

As governor, Haley resisted removing the Confederate flag from the state capitol until nine black church parishioners were murdered by a white supremacist in Charleston, South Carolina. She's out.

Even if Trump stashed boxes of state secrets in his Mar-a-Lago bathroom and refused to return them to the National Archives, as charged, he's committed another crime for which he can't be prosecuted.

Trump poisoned the well, corrupted and even destroyed the "grand old party" for a generation or two. He never chose someone for a smooth succession, like most leaders try to do, because of his lust for power.

Instead, he incited a mob to hang Vice President Mike Pence on Jan. 6, 2021, in the coup gone wrong. The gallows was set and ready outside the Capitol.

Pence did the right thing on Jan. 6, 2021, to defend democracy. He refused to let the armed mob attack on the

Capitol keep Congress from finishing the electoral count in the wee hours. The genteel Pence broke with Trump after meekly following him for years.

Yet the Indiana man is an arch-conservative.

Torn, I turned to Norm Ornstein, the sage of Washington politics, for his opinion on the best Republican running. He named a dark horse in the race:

"(Former Arkansas Gov.) Asa Hutchinson has more intellectual honesty than the others. Having said that, of course, he is extremely conservative and would pick radical right-wing judges and be bad for abortion and many other issues. But I believe he'd support the rule of law."

The refreshing rule of law. He's in.

From Capitol to Courthouse: Like a Vision

Aug. 9, 2023

WASHINGTON—The truth is getting lost already, as always when former President Donald Trump enters the room—or a courthouse.

Since the wrong crowd came to town on Jan. 6, 2021, our city longed for a moment of truth after the Trump mob stormed the Capitol. A Thursday on an August afternoon brought a fleeting moment of justice for that bleak day lasting into night and morning.

Make that mourning.

Fleeting, because Trump and his president's men are now waging a series of lies, threats and character assassinations to fire up his base of followers. And they are base. Lawyer John Lauro uttered a falsehood his first day in court, which went unchecked.

In the press room in that federal courthouse for Trump's Jan. 6 indictment, the mood was silent and grave as we watched a livestream. Special counsel Jack Smith caused a ripple when he walked in to watch, his stern, bearded visage fixed.

Then came the chilling familiar figure with the long red tie, sauntering and churlish as usual. Courtrooms are nothing new to the real estate mogul, who lived and breathed lawsuits in New York.

In a twist of poetic justice, the magistrate speaking coolly down to the defendant was a woman. After a greeting, she addressed him: "How old are you, Mr. Trump?"

Oh, he didn't like that. "Seven seven." Even less, her failure to call him "President Trump." He was seething, fit to be tied.

The federal judge in the actual trial will be Tanya Chutkan, a distinguished Black jurist who's presided in several Jan. 6 cases. Knowing the contempt Trump feels for Black women—he had virtually none among his appointees—will surely spice the courtroom drama with bitter herbs. Judge Chutkan showed her chops by promptly ordering a hearing on a protective order this week.

On offense, Trump is trying to get another trial judge, time and place, like maybe West Virginia.

To witness an ex-president go through a criminal proceeding, warned not to intimidate witnesses, was sweet sorrow. It was a moment in time and history that could never be undone.

Not to be outdone, Trump immediately began to intimidate witnesses, in capital letters: "If you go after me, I'm coming after you!" Prosecutors were unamused at this possible abuse of the First Amendment. The liberty and limits of free speech are at stake here.

This was Trump's third indictment. Conspiring to block the peaceful transfer of power carries the most weight in American democracy. President George Washington showed how it's done, when he likely could have stayed for life.

In 45 pages, the sordid story is laid neatly upon the table for Trump and his "crackpot" lawyers, as former Vice President Mike Pence put it. "Too honest" is what Trump said about Pence, according to charges.

The day in court was personal, a vindication for those who saw that day within the Capitol walls, who heard breaking glass, footsteps pounding, grunts and cries, gunfire in the Speaker's Lobby.

A seasoned journalist and Pulitzer Prize winner said to me outside the courthouse, "I'm still angry for the young staffers who were terrorized," hiding beneath desks and in locked bathrooms in senators' hideaways.

We rushed down a secret staircase through tunnels, breathing hard, hoping not to meet the mob head-on. There were 30,000 of them, way outnumbering us.

Now Trump is crossing swords with Justice, the department that moved slowly but picked up speed with Smith. He also indicted Trump for hiding state secrets in boxes and sharing classified documents after he lost and left office.

Most worrying: Trump's ferocious attacks on Smith, who prosecuted war crimes, as "deranged." His method of disinformation is devilishly simple. Trump truly believes that repetition is the golden goose of making people loyal to his version of events.

Unfortunately, there's truth to that. He learned his lessons well from a vicious mentor, Roy Cohn, lawyer for Sen. Joseph McCarthy during his 1950s "witch hunts" — how Trump first learned his favorite term.

Smith will keep his own counsel, properly mum, while Trump's voice blares in the public square and on the presidential campaign trail as he faces three trials. He's turning his troubles with the law into populist virtue, taking one for the team, or something like that.

A victim of political persecution, not prosecution.

The American public is not used to silent dignity after our Trump nightmare (from which we're trying to awake.) I do not regard him a legitimate president, but a black blot on the record that far exceeds Richard Nixon's Watergate scandal, leading to his resignation many Augusts ago in 1974.

When I went to my goddaughter Clemency's wedding in England back in 2018, all I could say to bewildered friends in the garden was, "I apologize."

In recent days, Trump expanded his vengeance to the American women's soccer team for losing to Sweden in the World Cup, blaming them for being too "woke.' He lashed out at House Speaker Emerita Nancy Pelosi ("a wicked witch") for her remark that he was a "scared puppy" on his way to the courthouse: "How mean a thing to say!" Poor Donald; she gets to him more than anyone.

He had harsh words for the nation's capital, saying it looked poorly since he left office. Somehow the temple of the Lincoln Memorial survived without him.

In the subversive "Barbie" movie manifesto, Trump may be central casting (off-camera) as Patriarch-in-Chief. His appeal lies in doing and saying the unthinkable. He brings out the worst in angry white people who feel their rightful place in the social order—and their control over others like women, Blacks, gays, immigrants and every Democrat under the sun—is under threat.

Liberals often make the mistake of framing Trump as absurd even as he hints of more civil war to come. He is a dangerous man. Taunting a judge to rein in his language is his first act in the drama of democracy, *itself on trial.*

A Florida lawyer, Lauro has a brazen edge. He exclaimed in court, "The government's had three and a half years" to build their case. In fact, the Jan. 6, 2021, attack took place two and a half years ago. But who's counting the time besides me?

On the Sunday talk shows, Lauro, 61, kept referring to his client's conspiracy indictment as a "Biden administration" move. Clever yet deceptive, making it hard for interviewers to interject. Planting that seed into public discourse further poisons it in a deeply divided nation.

When will we heal from Trump's barrage of lies, boasts, insults—and a medieval onslaught on uniformed police?

The citadel of the Constitution was violated like never before. The British burning the Capitol in 1814 was within the code of war by a nation's army of redcoat soldiers.

The Metropolitan Police Department, 800 on the scene, saved us from the mob. "I'll always be thankful," I told an officer Thursday. There they were, a host of a hundred lined up like they were on wintry Jan. 6.

Seeing the Capitol's marble dome as I emerged from the courthouse in summer rain was a vision: something sacred as the Wailing Wall, besieged but still standing.

Jamie Stiehm

In Trump They Trust: Bread and Circuses

Aug. 30, 2023

WASHINGTON — An ancient Roman poet foresaw former President Donald Trump as a deposed ruler raging to regain power: in a famous line, with "bread and circuses."

Master satirist Juvenal poked at corruption in Rome's leaders. Yet he also aimed his pen at the people, who lost their right to govern the proud Roman republic.

They surrendered citizen status in the rise of the Roman Empire.

Here in federal court, Judge Tanya Chutkan — and special counsel Jack Smith — are the noblest Romans of them all for bringing Trump to face justice.

Over his lawyer's shouts, Trump's trial for trying to steal the 2020 presidential election is set for March 4, 2023.

Back in ancient Rome, the common people, the masses fell prey to a cynical political strategy, "bread and circuses."

Translated from the Latin: "Keep 'em fed with free grain and let 'em watch gladiators and amusing contests to their hearts' content." It was a way to distract people, keep them nice and quiet.

That's what I see in Iowans and other Trump voters at August state fairs. There's barbecue beef and harvest corn to go round and round, and well-fed farm animals with ribbons round their necks.

"Iowa Stubborn" fairgoers are mesmerized by Trump's political circus, as if cast in a spell.

This state of mind has little to do with issues.

My father, a Wisconsinite, wonders how sensible Midwesterners can be stubbornly loyal to a man with four criminal indictments.

That is the question we must ask, and not just in red state diners in Ohio, where cable correspondents seek voter wisdom.

We need to get at the heart of why so many Republicans are blind to the brutal Roman emperor in Trump. After all, he's no Julius Caesar. And at least Nero could play the fiddle.

The answer: Trump invites the darkest sides of our selves to come out to display. The greatest leaders, like Franklin Delano Roosevelt, lift the best in us.

History will note Trump put the "coarse" in public discourse — the American character and conversation.

Acting out, Trump appeals to the worst gut instincts — in whites, mostly — who voted for him out of grievance, unwilling to accept a woman president after a Black one.

(If only Barack Obama tried harder to get Hillary Clinton elected, but that's a story for another day.)

There is no difference between the private and public vulgar Trump. He makes manners seem a thing of the past. I for one appreciate class, cheer and courtesy in a president.

The only comfort is that Trump lost the popular vote twice and won't pick up new voters in 2024.

The armed mob violence he unleashed in 2021 was near-death for American democracy. I witnessed the siege within the walls of the Capitol.

Our neoclassical Capitol evokes the majesty of the Roman Senate and Republic.

Trump has no book-learning about the ancient world, but a canny grasp of appealing to the lowest common denominator in people. He practices that in Iowa, New Hampshire, wherever he may be. He has zero respect for hallowed ground or institutions. Early on, he called the White House "a dump."

His defiant, self-aggrandizing speeches ramble on with no script. But he has a ringmaster's command, which Juvenal would appreciate.

Then Trump flaunts and parades his shameless language and actions, over and over, amplifying lies, boasts and insults day and night on his "social" media. *How juvenile, pardon the pun.*

Remember the Muslim ban on travel? Then the white supremacy rally in Virginia full of "very fine people"? Trump was just getting warmed up.

Back in New York, his fake Time magazine covers, his begging to go to Chelsea Clinton's wedding, his callous treatment of women (including wives) were steppingstones in a ruthless quest for image-building.

Trump's swagger is not so proud now that his mug shot was released in Atlanta. He's charged with conspiring to undo the Georgia state 2020 presidential election.

Sen. Robert C. Byrd once observed that the fall of the Roman Republic and the rise of Empire resulted in "a turbulent stream that flowed through dark centuries" of conspiracy and violence.

Let's not go there. That history path must stay past.

Justice For a January Day, At Last

Sept. 6, 2023

WASHINGTON — Enrique Tarrio, leader of the extremist Proud Boys, came to the federal courthouse to be sentenced for seditious conspiracy (and other counts) committed on Jan. 6, 2021.

The violent Trumpist Proud Boys were first to march to the Capitol, even before former President Donald Trump sent the mob of thousands to assault police lines and storm the sacred citadel.

Inside the House chamber, we heard howls and shrieks, footsteps pounding, breaking glass on marble floors — and then gunshots just outside in the Speaker's Lobby.

Yes, I was there.

Suddenly, a formal ritual — Congress counting presidential votes — turned into a siege of the House and Senate. The violation of the Constitution was stunning, to this day.

Everyone ran for their lives during the rampage. For the first time, American democracy's peaceful transfer of power failed. Plain and simple, it was an attempt to turn the 2020 presidential loser, Trump, into the winner.

The mob caused 150 police casualties in hand-to-hand combat. About a thousand arrests have taken place, according to the FBI.

Government lawyers said scores of Proud Boys were a "tidal wave in a sea of rioters" in the ironically named Peace Circle. At the end of the January day's mayhem, Tarrio bragged about his ranks street-fighting the police and vandalizing the Capitol:

"Make no mistake, we did this."

On the week of the attack, Tarrio was under orders to stay out of the city, after he pleaded guilty to burning a church's "Black Lives Matter" banner. The jury found he commanded the conspiracy, in touch with co-conspirators from nearby Baltimore on Jan. 6.

Tarrio and the Proud Boys started plotting the Jan. 6 Capitol attack as early as mid-December 2020, Judge Timothy Kelly stated. Pepper spray and armor was part of the plan. They coordinated with the militaristic Oath Keepers extremist group, led by Stewart Rhodes, in tearing down barricades.

Rhodes is now serving an 18-year sentence.

Tarrio fully intended for the Proud Boys to use force against the government, the judge declared. Affirming that Tarrio was the ultimate leader in seditious conspiracy, Kelly handed down a sentence of 22 years.

Tarrio's sentence is the longest given to any Jan. 6 defendant. Trump himself goes on trial in this very courthouse on March 4, for election interference.

That January day, if the plan worked, would be a triumph for Trump, and a resounding win for violent extremists, leaving the ship of state in limbo.

Lawyers for Tarrio told the judge he was a "misguided patriot," a Miami native with Cuban-American heritage.

Seeing his overwrought mother in the restroom for three seconds, I shed no tears.

Jan. 6 was not the Proud Boys' first time in the public eye. In Charlottesville, Virginia, in 2017, a white supremacy march turned deadly. Authorities consider it a white nationalist, racist, misogynist and violent all-male group.

Trump treated the Proud Boys as foot soldiers at his beck and call. "Stand by," he addressed them during a presidential debate.

The Anti-Defamation League closely monitors the Proud Boys and predicted violence would break out on Jan.6, 2021. Law enforcement was mostly caught by surprise.

The Metropolitan Police Department—800 officers—saved us.

I went down to see the convicted 39-year-old face his fate. Slight, bald and bearded, Tarrio was clad in an orange jumpsuit.

This guy had thousands of followers? This guy rounded up a ragtag army to report from all over the nation?

This guy plotted a constitutional crisis?

Oh yes, believe it.

"This trial has humbled me," Tarrio said. He apologized to police officers injured in the melee and to citizens of Washington.

"I was my own worst enemy," Tarrio said, showing regret for comparing one Proud Boy to George Washington. He asked Kelly to show him mercy.

Prosecutors requested 33 years. The defense requested 15. Tarrio will age to about 60 in prison.

As we in the press room awaited for the judge's sentence, a famous line from "The Godfather" came to mind.

The character Michael Corleone (Al Pacino) delivers it: "It's not personal, Sonny — it's strictly business."

Enrique, between us, Jan. 6 was personal. I witnessed the winter crime and now your punishment on a bright summer day.

About the Author

Jamie Stiehm's journalism career spans CBS News in London, the Baltimore Sun and The Hill newspaper in Washington. In her Creators Syndicate column, she covers national politics and history. She is also a public speaker on Anerican history and witnessing the Jan. 6th storming of the Capitol. Jamie lives in Washington. Her work is collected on JamieStiehm.com.

The War Within
is also available as an e-book
for Kindle, Amazon Fire, iPad, Nook and
Android e-readers. Visit
creatorspublishing.com to learn more.

∘ ∘ ∘

CREATORS PUBLISHING

We find compelling storytellers and
help them craft their narrative,
distributing their novels and collections
worldwide.

∘ ∘ ∘

Made in the USA
Middletown, DE
13 September 2024